*Putting My
Dress-Up Clothes Away*

Putting My Dress-Up Clothes Away
Because Big Girls Live in the Real World

Martha Bailey

Insight Press
Covington, Louisiana

Insight Press, Inc.
P.O. Box 5077
Covington, Louisiana 70434

© 2007 by Insight Press
All rights reserved. First printing 2007.
Printed in the United States of America.

No part of this publication may be reproduced, stored in a retrieval system, or transmitted in any form or by any means—electronic, mechanical, photocopying, recording, or otherwise—without the prior written permission of the publisher.

Library of Congress Cataloging-in-Publication Data
Bailey, Martha, 1950-
Putting my dress-up clothes away : because big girls live in the real world / Martha Bailey.
p. cm.
ISBN 0-914520-47-4 (alk. paper)
1. Christian women--Religious life. 2. Christian women--Conduct of life. I. Title.
BV4527.B25 2007
248.8'43--dc22
2007007275

Unless otherwise stated Scripture quotations are taken from the HOLY BIBLE, NEW INTERNATIONAL VERSION. Copyright © 1973, 1978, 1984 International Bible Society. Used by permission of Zondervan Bible Publishers.

Other quotations are from the KING JAMES VERSION and THE MESSAGE. Scripture taken from THE MESSAGE. Copyright © 1993, 1994, 1995, 1996, 2000, 2001, 2002. Used by permission of NavPress Publishing Group.

To my precious family:
Waylon, Anna, Emily, Chris, Brad, Jake, and Chase,
my treasures whom I love with an indescribable love—
I dedicate this book.

Without your love, support, and encouragement
this book would have never become a reality.
Thank you for joining me on this journey.

"For this reason I kneel before the Father, from whom his whole family in heaven and on earth derives its name. I pray that out of his glorious riches he may strengthen you with power through his Spirit in your inner being, so that Christ may dwell in your hearts through faith. And I pray that you, being rooted and established in love, may have power, together with all the saints, to grasp how wide and long and high and deep is the love of Christ, and to know this love that surpasses knowledge—that you may be filled to the measure of all the fullness of God."
—Ephesians 3:14-19

Table of Contents

Acknowledgements 11
Introduction 13
1: Putting My Dress-Up Clothes Away 15
2: The Elevator 19
3: The One with the Power 22
4: Love in Action 26
5: Making Memories 31
6: Rx for Joy-Impaired Women 34
7: Plans for You 39
8: Twenty-Five Cent Word 43
9: Six-Foot King Snake 47
10: Company's Coming 52
11: Eating with the President 56
12: Sunrise over Haleakala 61
13: Dumb, Really Dumb 64
14: I Just Can't Get That Off My Mind 67
15: Just Like Daddy 71
16: The First Big Blowout 74
17: You Want Gucci? No Problem! 77
18: A Crying Shame 80
19: Fiasco in the Ladies' Room 84

20:	Lemons but not Lemonade	89
21:	The Peacemaker	94
22:	Dirt in Her Baby's Eyes	97
23:	Church, Hawaiian Style	101
24:	Can I Just Write Her Off?	105
25:	The Mystery of the Lost Purse	110
26:	Watermelon Coin	115
27:	Turn the Light Back On	119
28:	Flip-Flops and God's Name	123
29:	The Big Birthday Party	126
30:	My Little Angel	130
31:	Burning Coals on Her Head	135
32:	Snake in the Bush	138
33:	Proud Mama	142
34:	The Ugliest Dress I've Ever Seen	147
35:	Foolish Pride	152
36:	The White Out	157
37:	Pooh Friends	161
38:	"Honey, You Must Need a New Battery"	166
39:	A Bouquet for Jesus	170

Acknowledgements

My heart is overflowing with gratitude for so many people without whom this book would have never gone to print. While my name is on the cover, the real authorship belongs to all those who have made an indelible imprint on my life—the young adults in my Bible study classes over the past seventeen years, the precious ladies in my church who have indulged me by listening to most of the stories I have shared in this book, and the wonderful teachers who have enriched my life since birth. Over the past few years, I have had the privilege of delving into God's Word through the writing of gifted teachers such as Beth Moore and many others. I am most grateful.

Since the first moment I entertained the idea of writing, God has sprinkled people along my path like bread crumbs for Hansel and Gretel—each one following the other just closely enough to keep the idea before me. Thank you, Bunny, for your persistent but gentle nudges to consider this endeavor. God has used you in more ways than you will ever know.

Thank you, Prayer Angels—Cindy, Mary Ann, Carolyn, Theresa, Elna, Yvonne, Tissie, Amber, Candy, Cleta, Susan, Dawn, Lynne, Anna, Tommie, Lynn, Linda, Terry, Kim, and Darlene. Your faithfulness not only in your prayers but also in your words of encouragement has sustained me throughout the entire process. Others of you have prayed for me as well. I appreciate you just as much. Lucy, your impeccable eye for detail coupled with your relentless desire for perfection have been invaluable to me.

The most special part of the whole process has been the quality time my family has invested in this project. You have worked tirelessly and joyfully and have constantly encouraged me to persevere. Anna and Emily, I have cherished every minute this book has brought us together whether in person, on the phone, or through email. Chris and Brad, I have felt both affirmed and encouraged by your enthusiasm and helpful suggestions. Waylon, I have counted on you to be my theological coach and honest critic. God did a wonderful thing when He placed you in my life.

But when it's all said and done, the praise, honor, and glory go to our Lord and Savior Jesus Christ. I gratefully acknowledge Your love, strength, and inspiration, Father. May You be glorified through every page of this book.

Introduction

How honored I am that you have chosen to allow me to direct your thoughts over the next few days, whether you read the book straight through or read it as a devotional guide. Throughout the pages of this book you will find stories about my family, along with stories about other people and events in my life as well. Some are as recent as the book itself while others go all the way back to my childhood.

All the stories are true with only the tiniest bit of embellishment. As you probably know, human nature doesn't need to be embellished. We are quite colorful enough on our own. On most days no standup comedian is needed to help those around us to have a good laugh. However, much of life isn't funny. It's painful, stressful, and heavy. Just as it takes peaks and troughs to make a wave, so it takes funny times and serious times to make life. Having worked with women for the past sixteen years I know that we like to talk about both. We love to laugh with each other, and we also like to cry together. In fact, no women's get-together is deemed a success without tears of one kind or another.

To let you know that the person writing this book struggles with life just like you, I have included a few of my serious mess-ups that later became humorous (*at least to other people.*) I have also included some topics that I believe we need to frankly discuss. Reflecting on each memory, I have asked the Lord for a spiritual application for each one.

My prayer is that you will be both entertained and challenged as you read.

Chapter 1

Putting My Dress-Up Clothes Away

"Man looks at the outward appearance,
but the LORD looks at the heart."
—1 Samuel 16:7b

Scripture Reading
1 Samuel 16:1-13

We were having dinner with one of the deacon families from the church where my husband was pastor. The deacon's family was similar to ours—a husband, wife, and two daughters. The kids had already gobbled down their food and gone upstairs to play. The two older children were doing what preteens do—listening to music and talking. The two younger ones were playing dress-up.

Putting My Dress-Up Clothes Away

As the adults were finishing dessert, our friends' daughter and our Emily came flying down the stairs. Their daughter said with pride, "Look y'all, Emily is Cindy Lauper, and I'm a hooker from New York City!" It was one of those moments when you didn't know whether to laugh or cry. I suppose it had to do with whether or not you were the hooker's parents.

After our friends saw that we were not appalled, we all laughed together. They assured us that they didn't know where their daughter had ever heard such a term—much less learned how to dress the part. We assured them that they were not bad hooker's parents or anything like that. We teased them, saying, "Maybe it is true that the reason preacher's kids are so bad is because they play with deacon's kids."

This incident occurred many years ago, but I still chuckle when I think about it. The joke is that the pretend Cindy Lauper and the pretend hooker from NYC are now in the ministry, wonderful young women seeking to serve God with all their heart. Does God have a sense of humor or what?

Reminiscing about our girls playing dress-up makes me wonder—do big girls still play dress-up and pretend to be someone else? I think they do. They just do it more discreetly.

Psychologists tell us that an astounding number of women suffer from poor self-esteem and depression. Could this stem from our "dress-up syndrome"—the tendency to pretend to be someone that we are not? Why do we do that anyway? Is it because we constantly compare ourselves to other women and feel that we don't measure up?

I fear that often our expectations are totally unrealistic. The person we are trying to be doesn't even exist. Instead, she is an imaginary woman composed of the best parts of five or ten women—one woman's hair, another's eyes, another's hips, another's personality, another's teeth—I could go on and on, but you get the picture. When that happens, any woman is going to come up lacking. Who wouldn't?

Where did we ever get the idea that women have to look like Barbie anyway? Think about that for a minute. How ridiculous it is to let a less-than-one-pound piece of plastic make us feel inferior. Besides, have you ever really taken a good look at Barbie—I mean a really good look? Well, if you haven't, you need to. What you will discover is that she is nothing but bust and bones—two things that don't usually go together. If you don't believe me, try losing a few pounds and see where it comes off first—know what I mean?

Several years ago I heard that Barbie's figure is so out of proportion that if she were real, she wouldn't be able to stand up by herself. Would somebody please tell me what is sexy about a skinny blond who is so top-heavy she can't even stand up? (In case you are wondering, I am *not* jealous—well, maybe just a little.)

Many women in our society are hung-up on personal appearance anyway. Don't get me wrong. It's okay to look good. It's just not the most important thing. For example, King Saul was a handsome man—"an impressive young man without equal among the Israelites—a head taller than any of the others" (1 Samuel 9:2). However, good looks were all he had. He certainly didn't have a heart for God. That's why God rejected him as the king of Israel.

When Samuel searched for the next king, he thought that the first young man he saw was the perfect candidate. However, God said, "Do not consider his appearance or his height, for I have rejected him. The LORD does not look at the things man looks at. Man looks at the outward appearance, but the LORD looks at the heart" (1 Samuel 16:7).

Was God telling Samuel that personal appearance is not important? Of course not. He was saying that in order to be a person whose life really counts, there has to be more than a knockout appearance. While King Saul had a "to die for" physique, he didn't have a heart that matched it. He was dishonest, untrustworthy, and cowardly. His life didn't count for much other than his own selfish ambition.

In contrast, the person God sent Samuel to anoint as the next king of Israel was a little red-faced shepherd boy named David. What if David had said, "I can't be king of Israel. I'm not tall, dark, and handsome like King Saul. Why, he's a head taller than any of the rest of us Israelites. He looks like a king. Look at me. Do I look like a king?"

"No, David, you don't look like a king if you compare yourself to Saul," God might have said. "You never will. But I didn't create you to be like Saul. I made you to be you. I'm not even looking for a man who necessarily looks like a king. I'm looking for a man who *acts* like a king— a person with a heart like mine" (1 Samuel 13:14).

Let me ask you, are you striving to be the person God created you to be, or are you content to play dress-up for the rest of your life? Dress-up is for little girls. It's time for us to grow up.

Dear Heavenly Father,
It's such a temptation to compare ourselves with others, but I know that does not please You. Help me today to celebrate the person You created me to be. I'm a big girl now. I'm putting my dress-up clothes away.

Because of You,
Amen

Chapter 2

The Elevator

"A cheerful heart is good medicine."
—Proverbs 17:22a

Scripture Reading
Proverbs 17:22

Talk about embarrassing! *It was embarrassing.* "Come on!" I thought. "Don't these people know this elevator makes more than one trip per day—that it and the three other elevators will come back up if they miss this one?" My husband, Waylon, and I were at the Southern Baptist Convention in a large city. We were staying in a 50-story high-rise hotel downtown. Our room was on floor 30-something.

We got in the elevator to go down to breakfast before jetting off to the convention. It was comfortably filled when we entered, but after stopping on what seemed like every floor, it quickly became very uncomfortable. I grew tired of standing in the elevator like a penguin, so I carefully slipped one arm up and placed my hand on Waylon's shoulder.

The elevator moved to the next floor to pick up more passengers. I checked the weight capacity of the elevator, which was posted on the wall, and according to my estimate, we had exceeded the limit. Just as I finished my calculation, I looked *across* the elevator and much to my dismay noticed Waylon smiling at me. I looked at him, then down at my hand, and back at him. Realizing that I had my hand on another man's shoulder, I panicked! Boy was I glad that I had not squeezed what's-his-name's shoulder affectionately with one of those little love signals you give that no one else sees or understands.

But the fact remained. I had my hand on another woman's husband's shoulder and she was standing right beside him. I was hoping that she hadn't noticed. After all, shouldn't a woman's husband be safe at the Southern Baptist Convention, for crying out loud? But rest assured, what's-his-name had noticed. He was standing as lifeless as a statue, but his face was glowing like a 150-watt bulb—as was mine.

So what was I to do? My mind was working at warp speed. I thought perhaps I might handle it in such a way that only the three of us—Waylon, me, and what's-his-name—would know. Jerking my hand off his shoulder would be the worst thing to do. I decided to lift one finger at a time, thinking that perhaps he wouldn't even realize what was happening. That went pretty well, but there was one problem—once I had lifted all my fingers, how was I to get my hand back down by my side? In robot fashion I lifted my hand, and in right-angle moves finally got it back down by my side where it belonged.

I have no idea how Waylon and I got separated. That happened twenty years ago and I still haven't figured it out. *How* it happened I don't know, but it wasn't the least bit funny, not to me anyway. Waylon, on the other hand, was having a field day! He thought it was better than anything he had ever seen on ESPN. To make matters worse, he had the nerve to wink at me as if to say, "You go, girl!"

I thought to myself, "If I were close enough I'd do something I have never done to you—I'd slap that silly grin right off your face!" Not wanting to call anyone else's attention to the little episode going on in the elevator, though, I resorted to a "read my lips" form of communication. Without making a sound I said, "I am going to kill you!" (I'd like to think I didn't mean it.)

We finally made it to the lobby after what seemed like two days (probably 5 minutes max), and I decided the best thing to do was just get out of there hoping to never set eyes on this Baptist preacher ever again. Dream on, sister! Everywhere we went that whole week, what's-his-name was there. He would blush and so would I. And was that his only year to attend the convention? Noooo! I had to relive that whole experience every year.

Years later Waylon went to the SBC alone. When he got home, he said, "Martha, you have really done it this time. You know the preacher you were hitting on in the elevator? You caused him to change denominations. He's not Baptist anymore. He's Presbyterian."

What's the point of telling you this story? To make you laugh. Did I succeed? Studies have proven that a good laugh has great health benefits. Proverbs 17:22 says, "A cheerful heart is good medicine." What have you done that would give your family or your co-workers a good laugh today? Come on, laugh! Remember, it's good medicine.

Dear God,
Often we take ourselves much too seriously. Sometimes things just happen and all we can do is laugh. Thank You that You use certain experiences in our lives to serve as medicine for our souls. I pray that You can use this story of mine to lift someone's spirit today.

In Jesus' Name,
Amen

Chapter 3

The One with the Power

"For to me, to live is Christ and to die is gain."
—Philippians 1:21

Scripture Reading
Philippians 1:12-30

"Martha, would you call the captain off," she said emphatically, or at least in a way that indicated she wasn't teasing. "It's 11:30. We're tired and ready to go home. You're the one with the power on this boat," she added. I was shocked that it was 11:30—and more shocked that she thought I was the one with the power.

Eight of us had left the marina at 6:00 that summer evening headed across Lake Pontchartrain for dinner at a New Orleans seafood restaurant. It was my first trip in a boat with such nice amenities—two bedrooms, two baths, the works. I felt like Jackie O. to be perfectly honest.

As we clipped along across the lake, the conversation centered on the number of alligators that people see almost every night in the lake and especially along the marshes of the Tchefuncte River. Seeing that I was particularly fascinated with the conversation, the captain promised that he would show us tons of alligators (a little hyperbole) on the way back across the lake. I could hardly enjoy my dinner in anticipation of the alligator hunt.

As we headed back home everyone was out on the deck scanning the shoreline for red eyes. The captain had explained that alligators are easy to spot in the water because they appear to have red eyes at night. "There's one!" someone shouted. So off we cruised in hot pursuit. Unfortunately, it was only a red plastic cup. But being a seasoned seafarer, the captain was not the least bit disappointed. He knew full well that there were thousands of gators lurking in the swampy waters of the Tchefuncte River up ahead.

By the time we entered the mouth of the Tchefuncte after what seemed like only a few minutes, most of the crew lost interest in the gator expedition and made their way to the lower deck. It was when the captain meticulously steered us down the fourth little bayou about 11:30 that my friend (I think I am still her friend) pleaded with me to call off the hunt since I had *the power*. I realized she was not the only one weary from this adventure when I heard one of the other crew members mutter under his breath, "I'll buy her an alligator if we can just go home." So I said to the captain, "This has been so much fun, even though the gators weren't out tonight." He assured me that there would be other opportunities.

I still chuckle at the idea that I was thought to be the one with "the power" on board that night. Yet in reality, we all have power. Call it influence, impact, or any other name, but it's still power. Think about it. Who is it that you influence on a daily basis? Your spouse? Your children? Your friends? Your siblings? Your co-workers? People at church? People at the grocery store? The list could go on and on. Think about the vast number of ways you can influence others—facial expressions, gestures, tone of voice, opinions—whether in person, over the phone, through email and snail mail, text messaging, etc. Don't kid yourself. You have power! Yes, little ole you. Refusing to acknowledge it means you are fooling yourself and potentially living an irresponsible, reckless life.

Have you ever considered the difference you could make if every day you used your influence for the kingdom of God? Take Paul, a prisoner, for example—a man seemingly stripped of any kind of power or influence. Yet he realized that despite the fact that his body was in chains, no one could incarcerate his mind. He knew that no matter where he was, he still could have an impact on other people. Consequently he chose to use his imprisonment to witness to the Roman soldiers who guarded him every day. Listen to Paul's testimony about the impact one person acting responsibly had on other people. "Now I want you to know, brothers, that what has happened to me has really served to advance the gospel. As a result, it has become clear throughout the whole palace guard and to everyone else that I am in chains for Christ. Because of my chains, most of the brothers in the Lord have been encouraged to speak the word of God more courageously and fearlessly.... I eagerly expect and hope that I will in no way be ashamed, but will have sufficient courage so that now as always Christ will be exalted in my body, whether by life or by death. For to me, to live is Christ and to die is gain" (Philippians 1:12-14, 20-21).

Paul knew that while he could not change his circumstances, he could choose the way he perceived them. So instead of feeling sorry for himself and becoming more bitter and resentful by the minute, he chose to use his circumstances in a positive way. Look at the results. Not only did he help himself, he also had a powerful impact on the Roman soldiers who guarded him day in and day out—an opportunity, no doubt, he would have never had without being imprisoned. In addition to improving his own quality of life and witnessing to the Roman guards, he also motivated his Christian friends to courageously share the gospel within their sphere of influence.

What about you? Are you making any difference in your sphere of influence? Will America be any different because you—one person—were willing to use your influence in a positive way? Will the gospel be advanced because of you? Will your Christian friends be "encouraged to speak the word of God more courageously and fearlessly?" Do you have power? Absolutely! The question is, how are you going to use it today?

Dear Lord,
Sometimes I like to play the "little ole me" card so that I don't have to think about the responsibility I have for my influence. Help me today to be aware of every opportunity You give me to make a difference in my corner of the world. Help me to share the gospel with those who don't know You and encourage my fellow Christians to be more courageous in their faith.

In Jesus' Name,
Amen

Chapter 4

Love in Action

"But God demonstrates his own love for us in this:
While we were still sinners, Christ died for us."
—Romans 5:8

Scripture Reading
John 3:16-18

Are the words "I love you" the only way love can be conveyed? Of course not. In his book, *The Five Love Languages,* Gary Chapman says that each one of us has a preferred way of expressing love. For some people it's affirming words or physical touch, while for others it's giving gifts or spending quality time with the one they love. Most of us can easily identify with these ways of expressing love. But there's one more love language, according to Chapman—acts of service. Some people express their love by *doing* things for those they love. Let me give you an example by telling you about a little girl named Suzie.

Suzie was born into a very troubled family with three teenagers and an emotionally disturbed alcoholic father. Shortly after Suzie's birth her father lost touch with reality and was committed to a state psychiatric hospital where he resided for the next eighteen years—until his death.

At age thirty-five, Suzie's mom found herself alone with three teenagers and a toddler, and the responsibility of making a living for her family. She worked long, hard hours in a garment factory to make ends meet. Times were tough, but Suzie's siblings rose to the occasion and worked together as a team to care for little Suzie. While having a baby to care for seemed like the last thing the family needed, God somehow saw fit in His providence to allow this baby to be conceived amidst such stressful circumstances. One of her siblings told Suzie it was her birth that actually got them through those awful days when their father was first hospitalized. That made Suzie feel special, because she knew her siblings could have just as easily resented her birth. Suzie's siblings took care of her so their mother could make a living for the family.

Suzie remembers many times when her mother didn't have one penny left until the next payday, yet somehow they were able to make it from week to week. Suzie's mother left for work early every morning, but before leaving she always cooked Suzie a hot breakfast. If it was cold outside, Suzie's shoes were always warm because her mother had placed them on the space heater. These were just a few of the many loving things Suzie's mother did for her.

Do you see my point? Love is not necessarily what you say. It's what you do. Did you notice the loving care Suzie's siblings gave her? Did you note how her mother didn't abandon her and her siblings when things got tough? No, she did what she had to do to support them. Suzie's mother proved to her children that she loved them by her unselfish actions.

Suzie's father was placed in a hospital three hours away, but because her family did not own an automobile, the only time Suzie got to visit her father was when an uncle took her and her mother. That usually occurred once a year at best.

Suzie loved seeing her father when she was a little girl, but the older she got the more the reality of the situation sank in. Each visit became increasingly painful. While Suzie's siblings had many fond memories of their father before he became sick, Suzie had none. Suzie used to listen with envy as her siblings shared fun memories they had of their dad. She wished she could've been part of those memories because the only ones she had were ones from a locked security ward of a state institution. To this day she can still see the hand that unlocked the ward at the hospital where her father resided.

Although there weren't many pleasant memories from those eighteen years, there were a few visits with her dad that stand out in her mind. One occurred her senior year in high school.

On that particular visit, Suzie's family had finished their picnic lunch as usual. Her father, a smoker, pulled from his pocket a small Prince Albert tobacco bag. Everyone expected him to roll himself a cigarette, but instead he handed the bag to Suzie. Suzie, only seventeen and certainly not a smoker, didn't know what to do. Rather than upset him or cause a scene she took the bag and peeked inside. Much to her surprise there was money inside. In fact, there was a roll of money. "Where could Daddy have possibly gotten this money?" she wondered, but before she could come up with a logical explanation, her father interrupted her thoughts and said, "It's your college money. I want you to go to college. I have been saving it for years."

Realizing that her father had been saving most if not all the snack money the family had sent him for the past sixteen years was almost more than Suzie could handle. The roll consisted of mostly one-dollar bills—a sum of $113. Not much money even back then, but to Suzie it was worth more than a million dollars. It means even more today. It is securely tucked away in a safe deposit box at a bank. Do you know why? Because while Suzie never remembers hearing her father tell her he loved her, the money is tangible evidence that he did.

Perhaps you have already guessed that the little girl's name was not Suzie. It's Martha. I'm that little girl. This story is important to me because it reminds me that being loved does not depend on being told that I am loved. My family loved me. I know because they showed me by their actions.

The Bible is filled with examples of this kind of love—a love that is expressed in acts of service, not just warm fuzzy feelings or something you say. For example, Peter and John exemplified this kind of love when they healed the lame beggar who solicited money from them at the temple gate. Peter focused on the man and exclaimed, "Look at us.... Silver and gold I do not have, but what I have I give you. In the name of Jesus Christ of Nazareth, walk" (Acts 3:4b, 6).

The Bible says that "God is love" (1 John 4:16b), and Jesus was the epitome of what acts of service are all about—strengthening the legs of the paralytic, restoring sight to the blind, exorcizing demons from the possessed, giving food to the hungry, touching and healing the leprous outcast, just to name a few.

Jesus showed love for His disciples by the way He related to them on a daily basis. His ultimate expression of love for them was His defining action—His death. Paul said, "But God demonstrates his own love for us in this: While we were still sinners, Christ died for us" (Romans 5:8). The apostle John said, "For God so loved the world that he gave his one and only Son, that whoever believes in him shall not perish but have eternal life" (John 3:16).

Please don't misunderstand me. I'm not implying that saying "I love you" isn't important. It is very important. In fact the other day my four-year-old grandson, Jake, said, "Honey (that's my grandmother name), I love you all the way to heaven and back." Make no mistake—I will cherish that statement for the rest of my life. However, the words "I love you," without actions to back them up, are worthless.

If you're wondering whether someone loves you, look at what they do.

Putting My Dress-Up Clothes Away

There you will find your answer. Likewise, if you are seeking to express love to someone today, tell him or her, but remember what you *do* is just as important as what you *say*.

Dear God,
Thank You for being our Father. Thank You for telling us that You love us, but more importantly, thank You that You show us over and over. It is a privilege to be Your child and know that we can rest securely in Your love.

In Jesus' Name,
Amen

Chapter 5

Making Memories

"Who am I, O Sovereign Lord, and what is my family,
that you have brought me this far?"
—2 Samuel 7:18b

Scripture Reading
Psalm 127

"Bailey, you're making memories, and don't you forget it," the wise grandfather advised my husband as we hiked in the scenic mountains of North Carolina when our girls were small. Not having many pleasant childhood memories, it's a statement that keeps reverberating in my mind, making me determined to create every memory I can.

Life was tough growing up in a small town in south Alabama without a father in the home. My mother was a single working mom, and I was a latchkey kid before we ever knew what one was. I shudder to think now what could have happened to me. Thank goodness things back then were not like they are today.

Because Mother had to work, I spent a lot of time alone. The days were long and lonely. To pass the time, I watched television. Some of my favorite programs were *Leave It to Beaver* and *Father Knows Best*. As I watched those programs, experiencing family vicariously, I used to dream of having a family of my own. "When I grow up I'm going to have me one of those *real families* like the Cleavers," I'd say to myself. And do you know what? God fulfilled my dream and blessed me beyond anything I could have ever imagined.

I am married to the most wonderful man a woman could ever want. He is my knight in shining armor—my Prince Charming who carried Cinderella away into the sunset. Waylon is strong and has more integrity than anyone I have ever known. He has a pastor's heart, a passion for God, a love for people, and a contagious positive attitude. I love him so much. He's my best friend. He's a family man who practices his Christianity at church, out in the community, and, most importantly, at home. Thank you, God. You knew I needed him.

If that was not enough, God blessed me with two beautiful daughters—Anna, our firstborn, and Emily, our second. They have brought us indescribable pride and joy. I am so proud of the godly women they have become. I admire them so much. Their beauty is only surpassed by their character. Waylon and I haven't always gotten it right as parents—we've made our share of mistakes along the way—but the girls love us in spite of it, which means more than they will ever know. What a blessing it is to have them as friends now that they are young adults.

I prayed for strong men for Anna and Emily to marry, men who have a heart for God and who would love and cherish them. God answered that prayer. Anna is married to Chris, and they have two sons, Jake and Chase, with whom I am unashamedly smitten. Emily is married to Brad. They are newlyweds serving God in Christian ministry.

When you discover that God created family before He ever instituted the church, you realize how important family is to God. From the beginning, His design for the family was for one man and one woman to commit to one another for a lifetime and, in that context, bear children.

The Bible calls family and children, in particular, "a heritage and a reward from the Lord" (Psalm 127:3). Waylon, Anna, Emily, Chris, Brad, Jake, and Chase are my treasures. They are far too precious to ever run them down in anyone else's mind. I tell folks all the time, "My family members are not perfect, but the only way you'll ever know their faults is if you discover them on your own."

Of all the things we have had to do in ministry, the hardest by far has been to try to comfort those who have lost children. It has been during those times that I have realized more than ever what a treasure my family really is.

I hope you will cherish your family today and remember the advice our friend gave to Waylon about making memories. But more importantly, I want you to know that the Bible says, "Unless the Lord builds the house, its builders labor in vain" (Psalm 127:1a). It's only when we allow the Lord to be the architect, contractor, and foundation of our families that we can ever make the memories that will be pleasing to Him.

Lord,
I feel like David when he prayed, "Who am I, O Sovereign Lord, and what is my family, that You have brought me this far?" You have blessed me beyond anything I could have ever imagined. I thank You for my precious family. Apart from Your saving grace, there is nothing more important to me. I want You to be the architect, contractor, and foundation of my family, creating memories that I can cherish.

In Jesus' Name,
Amen

Chapter 6

Rx for Joy-Impaired Women

"Rejoice in the Lord always. I will say it again: Rejoice!"
—Philippians 4:4

Scripture Reading
Philippians 4:4-20

I picked up the phone, called Chris, my son-in-law, and told him I wouldn't pick up Jake that evening but would get him the first thing the following morning. After talking to Chris for a few minutes, I asked to speak to Jake. If you are a grandmother you can definitely appreciate the following conversation.

"Hey, Honey. Papa [his paternal grandfather] is mad," Jake confessed with a tinge of guilt in his voice.

"He is?" I replied, waiting to see where this conversation was going.

"Yes, and Grams [his paternal grandmother] is mad, too."

"She is?"

"Yes, she is."

"Well, Jake, why are Papa and Grams mad?" I questioned, knowing that he wanted to tell.

"I didn't stay in my bed [at naptime that afternoon]," he humbly confessed.

"You didn't?"

"No, I didn't. But, Honey, I'm happy. Are you happy, Honey?"

"Yes, Jake, Honey is happy." (Now are you ready for the next question?)

"Honey, are you coming to get me to spend the night with you?" he asked with the irresistible charm of a grandchild.

Knowing that I had just told Chris that I wouldn't pick Jake up until the next morning but also knowing that grandmothers are not good at saying no, I said, "Yes, Jake, I am. Let me talk to your daddy."

"Bye, Honey," he said, handing the phone to his dad.

When Chris got back on the phone he knew that I had done a 180-degree change of mind. He didn't say a word. I suppose he just chalked it up to my being smitten as a grandmother.

Jake was one happy little camper that day. There was nothing joy-impaired about that boy. He was joyful in spite of the fact that he had challenged the joy of everyone around him.

Let me ask you, are you joy-impaired? Are you always down or sad? Do you like to be that way? Seriously, do you like to be that way? It seems that some people actually do enjoy being joy-impaired. However, unless you are clinically depressed or are experiencing intense grief or pain, you don't have to be that way. Why? Because joy comes from having the Holy Spirit in your life. The apostle Paul said, "The fruit of the Spirit is love, joy, peace, patience, kindness, goodness, faithfulness, gentleness, and self-control" (Galatians 5:22-23a). That means we don't manufacture joy in our lives. Rather, it is a by-product of having a relationship with Christ, allowing Him to produce His fruit in our lives.

I am proposing a prescription today for those of us who are joy-challenged. This prescription requires the same type of regimen that you follow when taking an antibiotic. You must take it all—not half, not stopping and starting. You can't pick and choose. You have to take it all. Let's see what's involved.

First, you have to *choose* joy—you have to allow the Holy Spirit to produce it in your life. Several years ago I read a book entitled *Happiness Is a Choice*. The premise of the book is that if you want to be happy, you can be, but if you don't want to be happy, you won't be—plain and simple. Do you agree? Abraham Lincoln concurred. He said, "A man is just about as happy as he makes up his mind to be." Is that true for women? I think it is. But isn't it strange how some women just don't seem to want to be happy while others, in spite of extreme adversity, are some of the happiest people around? Why is that? It's because joy doesn't depend on circumstances. Thank goodness, because many times we don't get to choose our circumstances.

The apostle Paul would certainly vouch for that. When he wrote the Book of Philippians he was not aboard some luxury cruise ship in the Mediterranean. No, he was in Rome under house arrest, chained to an elite Roman soldier day and night. He was awaiting trial for a crime he did not commit. During this imprisonment, he wrote my favorite chapter in the whole Bible, Philippians 4. In it he gave his friends at Philippi a prescription for joy-impairment. He told them, "Rejoice in the Lord always. I will say it again: Rejoice!" (Philippians 4:4). Knowing his situation, what does that tell you about joy and circumstances? It tells you that if you want to be happy you have to choose it. The psalmist said it this way, "This is the day the Lord has made; let us rejoice and be glad in it" (Psalm 118:24). That's the first step in dealing with joy-impairment.

Second, in order to know true joy, you must *pray daily*. Paul said, "Do not be anxious about anything, but in everything, by prayer and petition, with thanksgiving, present your requests to God" (Philippians 4:6).

How's your prayer life? How often do you talk to the Father? What do you talk to Him about? Are your prayers basically a glorified Christmas list—gimme this and gimme that? A nonexistent or wish-list prayer life is a perfect setup for a perpetual state of joy-impairment.

Did you notice that Paul included thanksgiving when he talked to God about things that were on his heart? Gratitude is such an integral part of prayer. It brings sunshine into our lives. Being thankful is like opening the blinds in the morning to let in the light. It makes everything look so much better.

Paul said that instead of worrying we should pray about everything. And what did he say would result? Unexplainable peace. You see, joy and peace go hand in hand. Where you find one you find the other.

Third, if you are joy-impaired, you need to find yourself a *joy mentor*—someone who models true joy. John Ortberg teaches this in his book, *The Life You've Always Wanted*. I'm not necessarily talking about people who crack one joke after another, although they are fun to be around. I'm talking about a person who makes you feel better about yourself and life in general just to be around him or her. But I need to warn you about joy mentors—if you get up in a bad mood determined to have a really lousy day, they will foil your plans. Their goal is the opposite of yours. They wake up each morning determined to have a good day—they want to be happy, and they want everyone around them to be happy too. Their goal is to spread happiness wherever they go.

If you want to be happy, you must seek ways to be around people who are happy and minimize your time with people who are joy-challenged. If you don't, you will remain in a joy-impaired state for the rest of your life. Your fellow joy-impaired buddies will make sure of it. They will undermine any attempt you might make to break free. That's exactly why you need a joy mentor.

Finally, if you are joy-challenged but don't want to be, you have to *discipline your mind*. This idea is also from John Ortberg. Joy comes from

Putting My Dress-Up Clothes Away

what we think about. That's why, in Philippians 4:8, Paul told us to think about things that are true, noble, right, pure, lovely, admirable, excellent, or praiseworthy. If you fail to acknowledge that you can choose what you think about, you play right into the hand of Satan. It is one of his cruelest and most detrimental deceptions. I'm not talking about random thoughts that run through your head. You can't control those kinds of thoughts. They are the result of all kinds of sensory stimuli. However, you can control what you dwell on for hours on end, day after day, year after year. You must control those thoughts. If not, they will keep you locked in a perpetual state of joy-impairment.

Are you up for the challenge? Are you tired of feeling down in the dumps? Do you want to be free from joy-impairment? Are you willing to try this prescription—choose joy, pray daily, find a joy mentor, and discipline your mind—to see if it works? Come on. What do you have to lose? Would it matter if I told you that Jesus prayed for your joy shortly before he was betrayed? Listen to Him praying, "I am coming to you now [Father], but I say these things while I am still in the world, so that they [My disciples] may have the full measure of my joy within them" (John 17:13).

Loving Savior,
I am thankful that You care so deeply about Your children. You demonstrated Your concern just before You died, when You prayed for our joy. Thank You for leaving us a prescription for it in Philippians 4. Help me today to apply the prescription to my life in the way You have prescribed it.

In Jesus' Name,
Amen

Chapter 7

Plans for You

*"For I know the plans I have for you…plans to prosper you
and not to harm you, plans to give you hope and a future."*
—Jeremiah 29:11

Scripture Reading
Jeremiah 29:1-14

"I'm sorry we can't catch the phone right now, but if you leave your name, number, and a brief message we will get back to you as soon as possible," said the voice on my friend's answering machine. "Catch the phone"—that was a funny expression to me.

You will find that living in Louisiana is a little different from living in other states—actually it's a lot different. Along with "catching the phone," people in Louisiana also "make groceries." And on their birthdays they don't turn 40; they say, "I just made 40." The word "bring" is a synonym for "take." For example, instead of asking, "Do you want me to take you home?" they say, "Do you want me to bring you home?" Folks here are very loving and generous and always want to give you a little something

Putting My Dress-Up Clothes Away

extra—that's called *lagniappe*, pronounced LAN-yap.

When people from Louisiana come to visit you they "pass by your house." The first time someone told me that they had passed by my house, I asked, "Why didn't you stop?" They looked at me like I was crazy and said, "You weren't home."

"How did you know?" I questioned.

"Because I just told you I passed by your house," they would say with great aggravation. By the time I figured out that "passed by" didn't really mean "passed by" but "stopped by" our conversation sounded like an episode of The Three Stooges. I didn't know if I was Larry, Curly, or Moe.

The names here are a little different too. I grew up with names like Smith, Jones, Johnson, Taylor, and so on. Here? The names are Leblanc, Peltier, Boudreaux, Breaux, and Thibodeaux, and those last three sound like they end with an "o." Go figure! And, oh yes, I must not forget Hebert—pronounced *ay-bear* not *hee-bert*.

Growing up in Alabama, I ate my share of hamburgers and enjoyed them immensely. In Louisiana we have burgers too, but the most popular sandwich is a po-boy—it's made with two pieces of French bread and almost anything you want to put between them. When you go to a restaurant here and order a burger or a po-boy, the server will ask, "Do you want that dressed?" The answer would be yes, if you want lettuce, tomato, pickles, and onions in addition to the regular condiments. We love to watch newcomers' faces the first time they are asked, "Do you want that dressed?"

The real kicker came one night at church when we first moved to Louisiana. It was a Wednesday night at what Baptists call Prayer Meeting. A voice from the back of the church said, "We need to pray for the Boudreaux family because John caught a heart attack and died."

"She didn't say what I think she said, did she—that he *caught* a heart attack?" I questioned—to myself, of course. Now, I was used to referring to someone who has a cold as "catching a cold" but not a heart attack. My initial response was to laugh out loud. I'm so glad I didn't because this was a very serious prayer request.

Now go back and read that sentence about John catching a heart attack, but before you do, you need to know how to say "John" in Louisiana. First squinch your lips together like you are making a fish face. Now say "John," and finish the sentence. You got it!

But that's not all. Get this. After the prayer request was made for John (did you say it right?) the person went on to say that the wake would be held the next night. Wait just a minute! Time out! I am confused! Didn't she just say he died? "Then there's no need to try to wake him up," I thought. "These people in Louisiana are nuts! How am I ever going to learn this culture?"

Little did I know that I had better get busy adapting to and learning the culture because God had plans for us to be in Louisiana a long time. You see, our plan when we first came to New Orleans was to stay three years, earn a Master's Degree, and return to Alabama. However, God had different plans. Some 36 years later we are still in the same vicinity. We laugh and say that God drove a stake in New Orleans, tied a rope around our ankles, and said, "You can go anywhere within a 60 mile radius." That's what we have done for the last 36 years.

I like God's plans. I can't imagine living anywhere else. This is home. I love it here. I love the people. I love the climate, even the humidity. I love the food—it is "some good!" I love jambalaya, crawfish pie, and filé gumbo, and all that good stuff Hank Williams sang about. And just think, it wouldn't have been the place I would have chosen. To live here was not our plan. It was God's plan.

In Jeremiah 29, the exiles who had been carried into captivity were encouraged to make the most of their time in Babylon. They would be there seventy years. Jeremiah basically said, "Bloom where you are planted." "Settle down," he told them, "build houses, plant gardens, bear

Putting My Dress-Up Clothes Away

children. Don't put your life on hold."

What about you? Are you really living where you live? No, that's not a mistake. I meant to ask it just like that. Many people are just biding time. They are not really living because they're longing for where they came from or where they'll be going. Don't do that. You will miss many blessings God wants to give you. You may be a minister's wife like me, the wife of a husband who gets transferred a lot, or a college student. My advice to you is to settle in and live—really live—where you are for however long you are there.

We laugh when people move to Louisiana from Texas because they come here dragging their heels all the way all the way from the Lone Star State. But guess what—they are the ones who cry the loudest when they have to leave. What irony!

"For I know the plans I have for you," declares the LORD, "plans to prosper you and not to harm you, plans to give you hope and a future."

Dear God,

I am so thankful that You had plans for us before we were ever conceived and that You reveal those plans to us little by little. Never in my wildest imagination did I dream that Your plans for my family would be in Louisiana. Oh, what we would have missed if we had been any other place. Thank You for the way You have blessed us here. Help me to be content here until You show us that You have other plans for us.

In Jesus' Name,
Amen

Chapter 8

Twenty-Five Cent Word

"For out of the overflow of the heart the mouth speaks."
—Matthew 12:34b

Scripture Reading
Matthew 12:33-37

Our girls are five and a half years apart in age. Anna is a typical firstborn, eager to please and easygoing. Emily, on the other hand, came here making up for lost time. Accepting the fact that she couldn't do everything Anna could do was hard for her. It caused her many frustrating moments.

One afternoon the girls were playing in the den when a domestic disturbance erupted. "You old E-pisto-palion!" I heard Emily exclaim at the top of her lungs. She was trying to call her sister an Episcopalian. No offense to those of you who are of the Episcopal faith. It was just that Emily had never heard that word until a few days before. Why she chose to use it in a derogatory way, we never could figure out.

Putting My Dress-Up Clothes Away

All in all, I'd say the relationship our girls had while growing up was rather typical for most families. By typical I mean they had their moments of hugging and kissing followed by moments of intense sibling rivalry. Family vacations were the time that behavior seemed to be the most pronounced. I'm sure being cooped up in the car for days only exacerbated the situation.

There's one trip in particular that stands out in my mind. As soon as we pulled out of the driveway, the duel began. The first controversy erupted over space. Each girl felt a need to claim her territory so an imaginary line, like the equator, was drawn down the backseat, equally dividing the space. Shortly afterwards, everything became "stupid this" and "stupid that," and they knew that they were going to be reprimanded every time I heard it. "Stupid" was on my bad word list. I certainly wasn't going to tolerate it for a week in the car.

Determining that verbal correction was not accomplishing my goal, I resorted to a more behavioral approach. Turning around and giving them what the girls always called "mama eyes," I stated authoritatively, "Girls, every time you say 'stupid' it's going to cost you twenty-five cents, and we are going to give the money to World Hunger." To make a long story short, let's just say there weren't very many hungry children fed by that fund. Except for one or two slipups, we didn't hear the word "stupid" the rest of the week.

Months later the girls were playing in the den when another heated argument broke out. At that point big sister Anna had the upper hand, and the little one had reached her frustration threshold. I heard Emily exclaim, "Anna, you make me so mad! I feel like calling you a twenty-five cent word!" Ascertaining that the situation might intensify to the next level and would involve a skirmish, I sailed into the den. The minute Emily caught sight of me she immediately started explaining. "I didn't call her stupid," she said defensively.

"That's right—you didn't," I replied. "But you and I know what you meant. Tell her you're sorry." Leaving the room I remember thinking that parenting was a much bigger job than I had ever anticipated. Not only did I have to police what my children said, but I also had to shepherd their hearts.

The writer of Proverbs said, "Above all else, guard your heart, for it is the wellspring of life" (Proverbs 4:23). You see, while inappropriate words often appear to be the problem, in actuality they are only a symptom. Jesus explained that the root of the problem lies in our hearts. "For out of the overflow of the heart the mouth speaks," He said. "The good man brings good things out of the good stored up in him, and the evil man brings evil things out of the evil stored up in him" (Matthew 12:34b-35). When it gets right down to it, our words are simply nothing more than expressions of our hearts. Garbage in and garbage out, they used to say, and I think that is precisely what Jesus had in mind.

James encouraged us to use our words responsibly. He said, "With the tongue we praise our Lord and Father, and with it we curse men, who have been made in God's likeness. Out of the same mouth come praise and cursing. My brothers, this should not be" (James 3:9-10).

Have you ever said something in anger and immediately wished you could take it back? Well, wish is all you can do because once a word is spoken it can never be retrieved. You can ask someone to forgive you, but you can never "unsay" anything. Once it's said, it's said. There have been times when I've been on the receiving end of someone else's unkind words, but even after a heartfelt apology it was very difficult for me to get over it. Contrary to what we would like to believe, kind words don't cancel or erase unkind words.

The Bible advises us to be sensitive, careful, and thoughtful with our words before we say them rather than having to be sorry, apologetic, and embarrassed afterwards. But don't ever forget that while our words are very important, they can only be as good as our hearts. Therefore, we need to pray as David prayed, "Create in me a pure heart, O God, and renew a steadfast spirit within me" (Psalm 51:10). What do your words reveal about your heart?

Dear Lord,
"Search me, O God, and know my heart; test me and know my anxious thoughts. See if there is any offensive way in me, and lead me in the way everlasting" (Psalm 139:23-24).

In Jesus' Name,
Amen

Chapter 9

Six-Foot King Snake

"Do not be afraid, for I am with you."
—Isaiah 43:5a

Scripture Reading
Isaiah 43:1-7

What would you do if you walked into your garage one morning and saw a six-foot snake as big around as your arm? Well, I can tell you what I would normally do—run like crazy and scream for Waylon. I hate snakes—any kind of snake! My mother was bitten by a cottonmouth when she was a child, and believe me, she instilled a fear of snakes in me that I'll never overcome.

On this particular morning, however, Waylon wasn't home—wouldn't you know! And while it was a shocking sight to see this six-footer in my garage, I wasn't totally surprised. When we first bought the remote property months earlier our only neighbor told Waylon about "the snake." "Make sure you don't kill our six-foot king snake," he advised, "because

Putting My Dress-Up Clothes Away

king snakes get rid of poisonous snakes."

Well, news about any snake wasn't exactly what Waylon wanted to hear. Knowing that country life was not exactly my cup of tea anyway, he dreaded having to tell me. Several days passed before he finally mustered the courage to break the news to me about the neighbor's snake. Needless to say, it didn't set too well. "Well, you can just tell Hal that if he doesn't want two nice three-foot king snakes, he had better keep that six-footer up the hill on his property," I said without batting an eye. But as you can see, our neighbor hadn't kept the snake up the hill, and now his prized six-foot snake was snooping around in my garage—much too close for comfort, I'd say.

It's a wonder that I had the presence of mind to do anything short of fainting when I saw the snake that morning. But miraculously, a bush hook was leaning against the wall nearby. In a flash I grabbed it and took several whacks at the snake (*Isn't it amazing what you can do when there's no one else there to do it for you?*), but unfortunately it got away.

Now I had a big problem, a really big problem! Realizing that my new neighbor was totally unable to keep *his* snakes on *his* property, I would have to live each day in fear. That's exactly what I did. Every day that fall when I stepped out of my house, I looked for the stupid snake. (Uh-oh! Twenty-five cents!)

Several weeks later, Waylon and I drove to a nearby city to pick up a dresser that we had refinished. When we got there the owner had a little grin on her face that neither Waylon nor I could understand. As soon as she saw us she said, "I bet you don't know what you had." Waylon and I were confused by the word *had*, but thinking that perhaps she meant to use the word *have*, we thought she might be insinuating that the dresser was worth more than we thought—maybe a priceless antique. Knowing that we didn't have a clue, the owner quickly explained. "When my guys started to work on your dresser, one of them pulled out the top drawer and a six-foot king snake slithered out! He turned white—and I don't mean the snake!"

Having no pity for the poor worker who could've had a heart attack on the spot, I couldn't help but think, "How clever I am—I honored Mr. Hal's request. I didn't kill his prized snake, but no one said I couldn't transport him thirty miles away!"

What kind of spiritual application can I make with this snake story? I think God has a word for us today about fear. Have you ever noticed how frequently we are told in Scripture, "Do not be afraid?" "Do not be afraid," the angel told Zechariah as he stood in the temple praying for a child (Luke 1:13). "Do not be afraid," the angel Gabriel told Mary when she found herself pregnant outside of marriage (Luke 1:30). "Do not be afraid to take Mary home as your wife," the angel told Joseph as he contemplated divorce (Matthew 1:20). "Do not be afraid," the angel said to the terrified shepherds out on the hillside tending their sheep (Luke 2:10). "Do not be afraid," the Lord told Paul when he was facing intense opposition at Corinth (Acts 18:9). "Don't be afraid," Jesus told Jairus, whose daughter was at the point of death (Luke 8:50). "Do not be afraid," Jesus told the anxious crowd who was worried about food and clothing—the basic necessities of life (Luke 12:32). "Do not let your hearts be troubled and do not be afraid," Jesus said to the disciples as his death became imminent (John 14:27b). "Do not be afraid," the angel told the women who went to anoint Jesus' body after His death (Matthew 28:5). "Don't be afraid," Jesus told the disciples as He walked on the water during a fierce storm on the Sea of Galilee (John 6:20).

It was not until August 29, 2005 that I learned to appreciate the story of Jesus stilling the storm and telling His disciples not to be afraid. Although I had read it many times I never knew how to apply it. Thanks to Hurricane Katrina, however, I now know Jesus as the One who can comfort me through the storms of life. While our lives were not endangered nor was our home totally destroyed during Katrina, our beautiful wooded area was devastated by the ravaging winds. It was a

Putting My Dress-Up Clothes Away

sight I still can hardly believe. It was surreal. Our yard took a beating, and looked like a place that had been bombed—forty-seven huge oaks and pines lying like pixie sticks on the ground.

For the first nine months after Katrina, practically every waking moment was spent either picking up debris or restoring damaged property. It was exhausting. As the 2006 hurricane season stared us in the face, we could feel the tension in the air. In the past we had bought a bottle or two of water, a few cans of soup, and some batteries when we knew a tropical disturbance was out in the Gulf of Mexico. Everything changed after Katrina. Because we now know what a category four hurricane can do, the people in Louisiana and the Gulf Coast are consumed with fear. If we're not careful, our entire summers will be lived in front of the television anxiously watching the Weather Channel, fearful of another storm as vicious as Katrina.

Does God want us to live our lives in fear? Absolutely not! Is life full of snakes and storms and a million other things to be afraid of? Of course. But rather than letting fear consume us, God wants us to confront our fears, trusting Him to take care of us. Listen to His reassuring words in Isaiah 43:1-5, "Fear not, for I have redeemed you; I have summoned you by name; you are mine. When you pass through the waters, I will be with you; and when you pass through the rivers, they will not sweep over you. When you walk through the fire, you will not be burned; the flames will not set you ablaze....Since you are precious and honored in my sight, and because I love you.... Do not be afraid, for I am with you."

God never promised that He would take the fearful times away, but He did promise to be with us through them. Which way will it be—fear or trust? The choice is yours.

Father,
The childish fear of the dark manifests itself in much more serious ways in our adulthood. It seems there are things to be afraid of at every turn, but I know

that You don't want us to be afraid. Thank You for Your reassuring words in Psalm 139:12, "Even the darkness will not be dark to you." Help me today to know that if You are not afraid of the dark things in this world, I don't have to be afraid either. Remind me that "When I am afraid, I will trust in you" (Psalm 56:3).

*In Jesus' Name,
Amen*

Chapter 10

Company's Coming

"Submit to one another out of reverence for Christ."
—Ephesians 5:21

Scripture Reading
Ephesians 5:21-33

Nothing, I mean *nothing*, was going to stop me. I was determined. Company was coming for Emily's high school graduation, and I wanted everything in the guest bedroom to be just perfect. The countdown had begun—seven days and counting. My work was cut out, but it was doable if everyone cooperated.

While the painter was hanging the wallpaper I was busily shopping for all the accessories. Because I planned to use white accessories with the blue and white toile paper, I felt very confident that I could pull it all together quite easily. The bedspread was already in hand—a white matelassé. However, there was a problem—the store where I had purchased the bedspread didn't have the pillow shams. But because there are hundreds—maybe thousands of Dillard's across the U.S., I knew the pillow shams could be located. Yep, they could. After a few phone calls, I found one sham in Baton Rouge and the other one in Shreveport, and they were being shipped to me as we spoke. The bedspread was actually a coverlet, which required a bed skirt but didn't come with one. My decorator friend suggested that we use a Battenberg lace bed skirt in the toile room with the matelassé coverlet. Perfect! I searched locally for the bed skirt but couldn't find it. The clock was ticking. I had to think fast!

Bingo! I thought of a solution. I had remembered seeing one in Foley, Alabama, at the outlet mall. It was only 3 hours, only 175 miles away—no big deal. Off I went to accomplish my mission. (Did I mention that I am a determined, persistent person?)

Oh yes, the furniture. It was ordered weeks earlier and was scheduled for delivery on the morning my guests were due to arrive. Why in the world I trusted that the furniture would be in, I don't know. But I did.

There was just one more detail that had to be attended to—the window treatment. I only wanted a simple valance, and guess where I found it? At Wal-Mart of all places. How lucky can a girl get?

Well, the day finally came. At 10 a.m. the furniture was delivered, but the bedrails didn't fit. So the deliverymen left and said they'd be back shortly. Seeing the fire in my eyes, they weren't going to let me down. And they didn't—they returned in an hour or so and finished setting up the bed.

When they left I speedily got to work. The first thing I did was put the Battenberg bed skirt that came from Foley, Alabama, on the bed. Next, I put on the coverlet, which came from Dillard's in Slidell. After putting on the pillow sham from Dillard's in Baton Rouge, I then put on the one from Dillard's in Shreveport. The finishing touch was applied when I hung the Battenberg valance that came from Wal-Mart. I walked to the door so I could get a good look at everything. I was very pleased. I even had one hour to spare before my guests arrived.

Putting My Dress-Up Clothes Away

Women! What strange creatures we are! If I didn't know better I might believe that women really are from Venus and men are from Mars, as author John Gray says, because the two sexes are so different. I do believe that if our guys could live without us they'd do it in a heartbeat. After God created man and saw how lonely he was, God said, "This is not going to work; man is going to die for lack of companionship." So God created woman. He brought her to the man, who exclaimed, "Oh, yes, I like this creature!" (This is from Genesis 2, with just a little paraphrasing!)

While we don't know what the conversation was between God and Adam, I think the following Indian legend which I read in the book, *We Can Have Better Marriages if We Really Want Them*, by David and Vera Mace, points out the need that husbands and wives have for one another. It also points out the potential for conflict. According to the legend, after only a week the man brought the woman back to the Creator God, Twashtri, and said,

> "Lord, this creature that you have given me makes my life miserable. She chatters incessantly, and teases beyond endurance, never leaving me alone: and she requires incessant attention, and takes all my time up, and cries about nothing and is always idle: and so I have come to give her back again as I cannot live with her." So Twashtri said: "Very well." And he took her back. Then after another week man came again to him and said: "Lord, I find that my life is very lonely since I gave you back that creature. I remember how she used to dance and sing to me, and play with me, and cling to me; and her laughter was music, and she was beautiful to look at, and soft to touch: so give her back to me again." So Twashtri said: "Very well." And he gave her back again. Then after only three days man came back to him again, and said: "Lord, I know not how it is: but after all, I have come to the conclusion that she is more of a trouble than a pleasure to me: so please take her back again." But Twashtri said: "...I will have no more of this. You must manage how you can." The man said: "But I cannot live with her." And Twashtri replied: "Neither could you live without her." And he turned his back on man, and went on with his work. The man said: "What is to be done? For I cannot live either with or without her!"

What a blessing marriage is! But, oh, how difficult it is sometimes to work together as a team. Because men and women are so different, we often butt heads and seem to pull in opposite directions, forgetting that we become "one flesh" in the marital relationship (Genesis 2:24b). As a result, we no longer function independently but interdependently. God created woman to be a companion—a helper—to the man (Genesis 2:18). God wants you as a wife to willingly submit to your husband just as He wants your husband to willingly love you like Christ loved the church and sacrificed Himself for it (Ephesians 5:22-25). This is God's ideal. Although it may seem old-fashioned, it works. And as the saying goes, "If it ain't broke, don't fix it." God's plan for marriage is for one man and one woman to live together for a lifetime, submitting to Him first and then to one another. What an incredible relationship we would have if husbands and wives could figure out how God intended for a marriage to work. How blessed we would be!

Dear Lord,
Next to You, my marriage is the best thing that ever happened to me. I praise You for giving me such a strong, loving husband and father to my children. I know that Your Word tells us how You want a marriage to work. Help me to willingly submit to Your authority first and then to my husband's. That's not always easy, but I know it is Your will. Help me to be obedient.

In Jesus' Name,
Amen

Chapter 11

Eating with the President

> "Train a child in the way he should go,
> and when he is old he will not turn from it."
> —Proverbs 22:6

Scripture Reading
Deuteronomy 6:4-12

"When people speak to you, hold your head up and look them in the eye."

"Put one hand in your lap; eat with the other."

"Don't talk with your mouth full."

"Chew with your mouth closed."

"Wipe your mouth with your napkin."

"Say please, thank you, I enjoyed my meal, and may I please be excused."

These were basic manners that we tried to instill in our girls when they were young. When they protested, I would end the discussion by saying, "You never know when you might be eating with the president."

Their response was, "Oh, Mom!"

Not long after Anna graduated from college and landed her first job, she called home one night. Her dad answered the phone. I quickly determined by his voice inflection and body language that Anna was telling him something very interesting. After a few minutes he said, "Anna, I'm going to hand the phone to your mom so you can tell her yourself." Talk about curious. I was curious!

After a brief hello, Anna said, "Well, guess what!"

"What?" I asked in a motherly way, trying to share the excitement of whatever it was that she was about to tell me.

"I ate with *the president* tonight." She waited for that to sink in, and then she continued, "The president of my company was in town, and I had dinner with him at a fancy restaurant."

"Well, how about that!" Then I jokingly inquired, "Excuse me, Anna, but do I hear a thank you for all those years I harped on manners and eating with the president?"

"Yes, Mom, you do."

"Did you know which fork to use and how to handle yourself?"

"Yes, I did. I appreciate all you taught me."

"Anna, could you repeat that? I didn't hear what you said."

"Mom, you heard me. You know exactly what I said."

"Okay, so I did, but I just wanted to hear it one more time."

I used to tell the girls that good manners won't ever go out of style—they will come in handy when you least expect it. I was vindicated that night at Anna's dinner party with *the president*. It was one of those proud parent nights—I was proud of my child, proud that she realized I had taught her something really important, and, yes, proud that she acknowledged it.

The Bible says, "Train a child in the way he should go, and when he is old he will not turn from it" (Proverbs 22:6). We usually think of this verse when it comes to the spiritual aspect of a child's life, and rightfully so. However, training a child involves every area of life—physical, mental, emotional, social, and spiritual. It's a huge responsibility—a 24/7 job with no days off or moments that don't count.

Everything we say to our children is important. However, the most powerful impact comes from our example. God made that crystal clear to us when we watched Anna brush her teeth as a preschooler. It wasn't so much the way she brushed her teeth but what she did when she finished. After rinsing her toothbrush under the faucet, she struck her toothbrush two times on the side of the sink to get the excess water out of it. Waylon and I looked at each other questioning why she would do such a thing. Then it dawned on us. She was merely mimicking what she had seen her mother do. It was as if God was saying, "Be careful. You are being watched. This little girl is going to do exactly what she sees you doing. In fact, what you *do* will be more important than what you *say*."

Training a child is about modeling—whether it's manners or a relationship with God. Most of the time children attach significance to the things that are important to their parents. If the parents value money, the children will be materialistic. If the parents value beauty, their children will deal with vanity. If it's fame, their children will desire notoriety. If parents value success, children will seek accomplishment. If parents value people, the children will value life. If parents value God, then children will value a relationship with Him. Values seem to be caught more than taught.

When I was in high school I had an English teacher who used impeccable grammar. I remember the first time I heard her say that when you answer the phone and the person on the other end asks to speak to you, you are supposed to say, "This is *she*." "This is *she*?" my classmates and I protested. We knew our teacher had to be wrong because everybody said, "This is *her*." Finally, after seeing that we were not convinced that she knew what she was talking about, our teacher opened the textbook and showed us the rule.

The interesting thing about the whole situation was that my teacher couldn't recite many rules of grammar. She just knew what was correct because she grew up in a home where her parents spoke near-perfect grammar. My teacher learned to speak correctly by mimicking her parents. What a sobering thought!

Think about the children you relate to on a daily basis. What are they learning by observing you? Are you setting a good example for them each day? Remember, it's not necessarily what you say that's important; it's how you live that really matters. It's not even a matter of how many Bible verses you can quote to your children. It's how they see you *applying* those verses to your everyday life.

James said, "Do not merely listen to the word, and so deceive yourselves. Do what it says. Anyone who listens to the word but does not do what it says is like a man who looks at his face in a mirror and, after looking at himself, goes away and immediately forgets what he looks like. But the man who looks intently into the perfect law that gives freedom, and continues to do this, not forgetting what he has heard, but doing it—he will be blessed in what he does" (James 1:22-25).

You will be blessed in what you do when you read and apply God's Word to your life. Your children will be blessed as well. The psalmist said, "The law of the Lord is perfect....trustworthy, making wise the simple....giving joy to the heart....giving light to the eyes" (Psalm 19:7-8). He went on to say that by observing the precepts found in Scripture we are "warned; in keeping them there is great reward" (Psalm 19:11). You see, the *Bible* will not only show you how to live, but it will enable you to be a good example as you train your children in the way they should live.

"Be careful. You are being watched. This little girl is going to do exactly what she sees you doing." Those were the words God whispered to Waylon and me more than twenty-five years ago. Do you hear Him whispering those same words to you today?

Dear Heavenly Father,

What a wonderful blessing children are! They bring so much joy into our lives, but what an awesome responsibility it is to train them in the way they should live. Father, You have reminded me today how important my example is in the training process. You have also reminded me that in order to be a godly example, I have to read, listen to, and obey the truth that is found in Your Word. Help me to read it and live it today for my children—and my own benefit.

In Jesus' Name,
Amen

Chapter 12

Sunrise over Haleakala

"This is the day the Lord has made; let us rejoice and be glad in it."
—Psalm 118:24

Scripture Reading
Psalm 19:1-6

"It's the most incredible sunrise you'll ever see. Trust me. It's worth getting up at 2 a.m. to see," the bellman assured the sleepy passengers as we boarded the van.

"All I can say is that it better be!" I thought to myself, hoping that we hadn't fallen into another tourist trap. Out of all the things to do on the beautiful island of Maui, we had been told that watching the sunrise over the Haleakala Crater was at the top of the "must see" list. We would know in a short time.

Since most of the tourists were half asleep, the two-hour trip to Haleakala was uneventful. Besides, there wasn't much to see as the van snaked its way up the volcanic mountain in the darkness. However, when we reached the 10,000-foot summit, everyone sprang to life. All the tourists scurried around getting suited up for the big event, pulling all sorts of winter gear out of their bags—heavy coats, woolen hats and scarves, and gloves. We had been warned that it would be cold, but I felt sure my jacket would suffice. I didn't think we needed to be dressed like Eskimos.

Looking around I noticed there were other tourists who hadn't even brought a light jacket. But don't think for a minute that bothered them! They just compensated for their lack of preparation by sporting blankets and comforters from their hotel room. One guy was even wearing a robe with the hotel logo prominently displayed on it. He didn't care. He was warm.

To say the least, we were a motley crew—all one hundred of us—but no one cared at that time of the morning. After all, we weren't there for a style show. We had come to witness an awesome display of God's splendor.

We knew the exact time the sun was going to rise because God created the sun to function in a predictable manner—and besides we had all watched the Weather Channel the night before. There was no chance that the big orange ball would sneak up on us.

Standing there on the observation deck was like experiencing the countdown before a shuttle launch, with each tick of the clock heightening the excitement and anticipation. As the horizon grew brighter and brighter, the hues of pink and red illuminated the eastern sky. Then all of a sudden like a jack-in-the-box the sun burst forth over the horizon just as scheduled by its Creator. It was an incredible sight to behold! All of us applauded spontaneously as if it were the first sunrise we had ever seen.

Not being a morning person, I don't usually get all that excited about the sun rising. I just take it for granted. What about you? Is it possible that our knowledge of astronomy and planetary science has caused us to lose some of the awe and wonder at what God does in our world on a daily basis? Would we be better off with a more simplistic understanding of the solar system like the people in the Old Testament had? They assumed that the sun rose each morning because God said, "Get up and do it again."

While I don't believe that God has to command the sun to rise each day, it is truly amazing how He created it along with the other parts of the solar system to function in such an orderly manner. How astounding it is that all of the gazillion stars, planets, moons, comets, and whatever else is out there move through the universe with such precision and predictability. And just think—God spoke all of them into existence. How awesome! "All things were created by him and for him" (Colossians 1:16b), "to declare the glory of God…to proclaim the work of his hands" (Psalm 19:1)—just as He created us for a purpose. It is truly mind-boggling!

Watching the sunrise over Haleakala Crater reminded me that each day is a gift from God—a gift to be appreciated and celebrated, not merely endured. How sad when our attitude is, "Just let me get it over with." Every day truly is the day the Lord has made, and we should rejoice and be glad in it (Psalm 118:24). The Bible tells us that our days are numbered (Psalm 139:16). That means we only have a certain number of sunrises, so make the most of this day! It's the last one like it you will ever have.

Dear Father,
You truly are the creator of heaven and earth. Nothing in this world is here by accident. Everything exists because of Your carefully orchestrated plan. Help me to treasure each sunrise, knowing that I only have a fixed number of them.

In Jesus' Name,
Amen

Chapter 13

Dumb, Really Dumb

"Do not judge, or you too will be judged.
For in the same way you judge others, you will be judged,
and with the measure you use, it will be measured to you."
—Matthew 7:1-2

Scripture Reading
Matthew 7:1-5

Have you ever done something dumb—I mean *really* dumb? Come on now, I know I'm not the only one. I'm talking about those things you do when you're not paying attention or don't have your mind on what you're doing. Let me give you an example.

Not long ago I was making a deposit at a bank we use only a few times a year. I drove to the window and crammed my deposit in the cylinder which was sucked up and over to the teller in a flash. The teller, obviously perturbed, said rather curtly, "Mrs. Bailey, this is not Bank XYZ. This is Bank ABC."

I was so embarrassed. It would have been bad enough to make a mistake like that in private, but the other four lanes of customers could hear everything she was saying. It was like she was announcing to the whole world or at least to the people in line, "Do you see this woman? She is crazy!"

What was I supposed to say? "Oops?" "Forgive me?" "Excuse me?" I don't remember what I said, but I do remember wishing the ground would open up and swallow me—car, deposit, and all.

As the teller was scolding me, I had a flashback to a few moments earlier as I pulled up to the bank. I remembered thinking, "What happened to the entrance? Why in the world did they change the driveway? The old concrete one was so much better. I hate this gravel stuff." For normal people—thinking people—that thought would have been enough to alert them to the fact something was not right about this situation. It would have been enough to shake them out of the stupor they were in, make them check their surroundings, and cause them to question whether or not they were at the right place. But not me. Instead of thinking I might have made a mistake, I went into a judgmental mode—questioning the bank's decision to change the surface of its entrance from concrete to gravel.

Perhaps that's what Jesus meant when he warned us about judging. "Do not judge, or you too will be judged. For in the same way you judge others, you will be judged, and with the measure you use, it will be measured to you" (Matthew 7:1-2).

Now, wait a minute—I think there is some inequity here! All I had done was try to make a deposit at the wrong bank. What's the big deal about that? Does that warrant being exposed to the world by an insensitive teller?

Jesus went on, "Why do you look at the speck of sawdust in your brother's eye and pay no attention to the plank in your own eye? You hypocrite, first take the plank out of your own eye, and then you will see clearly to remove the speck from your brother's eye" (Matthew 7:3, 5).

"You hypocrite"—oh my, that hurts! A hypocrite is a person who pretends to be something that she's not. When we judge others while pretending nothing is wrong in our own lives, we are being hypocritical. Furthermore, judging others is serious business to God. To show you just how serious it is, Jesus said we will be judged in the same way we judge other people. I don't know about you, but I don't want to be judged the way I judge others. Often I'm not very merciful. When I'm on the judge's bench I sometimes hold the bar much higher for others than I do for myself.

Perhaps my experience at the bank is a reminder to be on guard against a critical, judgmental spirit. There is nothing more unbecoming a Christian than to willingly and sometimes joyfully pick others apart. Instead of judging we are called to encourage one another. Paul exhorted the Thessalonians to "encourage one another and build each other up" (1 Thessalonians 5:11). I'm afraid that my hasty judgment at the bank that day was only the tip of the iceberg of sin that lay beneath the surface in my life.

What about you?

Dear Father,
It's so easy to point out the sin in other people's lives while I'm blind to my own sin. Help me today to be brave enough to allow You to reveal the areas where I need to repent and change. Forgive me for being critical and judgmental. Help me to treat others as I want to be treated.

In Jesus' Name,
Amen

Chapter 14

I Just Can't Get That Off My Mind

"And we take captive every thought to make it obedient to Christ."
—2 Corinthians 10:5b

Scripture Reading
Philippians 4:4-9

We often hear people say, "I just can't get that off my mind." What do they mean? Does that expression insinuate that we are helpless victims of our own minds? I think it does. But is it really true? When I read the writings of the apostle Paul in the New Testament, I don't get that impression.

Instead, Paul talked about *disciplining your mind*. "Do not conform any longer to the pattern of this world, but be transformed by the renewing of your mind," he wrote in his letter to the Romans, 12:2a. "Set your minds on things above, not on earthly things," he wrote in Colossians 3:2. "Take captive every thought to make it obedient to Christ," he exhorts Christians in 2 Corinthians 10:5b. All three verses are commands and indicate that we are not a victim of our thoughts. Unless we are going through intense grief or pain we can choose what we think about—that's what it means to discipline our minds. But how do we do it? Let's look at three very practical ways.

One way to discipline your mind is by *monitoring your thoughts*. "Take every thought captive," Paul said. That means that you need to pay attention to your thought-life. Do you realize that your mind is much like a gravel driveway? It, too, can develop ruts if you repeat the same thought pattern day in and day out. And over time, it's possible that the ruts in your brain, just like the ruts in your driveway, can get so deep that it is next to impossible to get out of them.

The reality is that after you have thought about certain things for a prolonged period of time, you train your brain to work by default. When you are not consciously directing your thoughts, your mind will automatically turn to certain subjects. Ask yourself, "What do I think about when I'm not deliberately trying to control my thoughts?" You might be surprised at how counterproductive your thoughts are.

Perhaps you have fallen into the rut of nonproductive thinking and don't even realize it. If that's the case, you must begin the arduous process of disciplining your mind by taking control of every thought. Invite the Holy Spirit to enable you to monitor your thoughts so you can get out of the rut of negative thinking. Replace those negative thoughts with ones that are true, noble, right, pure, lovely, admirable, excellent, and praiseworthy (Philippians 4:8).

Another way to discipline your mind is by *engaging in positive self-talk*—saying nice things to yourself. There's nothing wrong with it—after all, God did at the end of every day of creation. What did he say? "That's awful!" or "I really messed up big time today!" or "What was I thinking?" or "That is a sick color!" or "I really got carried away on the hippopotamus, didn't I?" No, He said, "That's good, in fact, that's very good" (Genesis 1).

Why then are we so reluctant to say nice things to ourselves? Is it because of the way we were raised? Were you taught that to think nice things about yourself was being conceited or proud? It can be—if you think that whatever you've accomplished was by your own doing. But if you have used your gifts and talents for God's glory, why shouldn't you feel good about that? I think God is pleased when you do.

Let's pretend you have a recording of everything you said to yourself yesterday. What would it reveal? Did you call yourself stupid? Did you berate yourself because of your looks? Is that the kind of self-talk your recording would reveal? Or is it possible that you affirmed yourself all day with positive, encouraging thoughts? That's the way it should be. That's healthy.

Several years ago I hired a serviceman to clean my sofa. After getting him squared away downstairs, I went upstairs. An hour later I heard him talking to someone. Knowing that only the two of us were supposed to be in the house, I was frightened at first. However, after walking to the top of the stairwell and listening for a moment, I discovered he was carrying on a conversation with himself. It was obvious he knew about positive self-talk when I heard him say, "Man, does that look good!" You see, he was saying nice things to himself. He had done a good job. He wasn't waiting for me to affirm him. He did it for himself. That's positive self-talk.

The third way to discipline your mind is by consciously *looking for reasons to laugh*. If you are like me, the best place to start is with yourself. For example, the other day I was ironing a pair of pants, but the iron kept sticking to them. "What's wrong with the iron?" I wondered. I had ironed those pants many times before and nothing like that had ever happened. Not only was the iron sticking, there was also a funny smell.

It wasn't a bad odor—actually it had a fresh, clean scent. Well, hello! My pants should have smelled really fresh and clean because I had been spraying them with bathroom cleaner instead of starch. (And for the record I don't think I infected anyone all day!)

Most of the time we take ourselves much too seriously. Rather than beat yourself up over silly things you do, laugh. It's good medicine, so the Bible says (Proverbs 17:22). And don't forget to tell someone else. They may need something to chuckle about too.

Remember: while you don't always choose every thought that goes through your head, you do choose what you dwell on. So why not choose to think good, clean, wholesome thoughts today? Get rid of those negative, nonproductive thought patterns that keep you bound in discouragement. Say nice things to yourself. It's okay. And consciously look for things to laugh about to help you discipline your mind.

Dear Lord,

Thank You that I don't have to be stuck in the rut of unproductive thinking and become a victim of my mind. Help me remember I can control what I think about by taking "captive every thought to make it obedient to" You (2 Corinthians 10:5b). Thank You for sending Your Holy Spirit to prompt and direct my thoughts. "May the words of my mouth and the meditation of my heart be pleasing in your sight, O Lord, my Rock and my Redeemer" (Psalm 19:14).

In the Powerful Name of Jesus,
Amen

Chapter 15

Just Like Daddy

"So God created man in his own image."
—Genesis 1:27a

Scripture Reading
Genesis 1:27-31

When Emily was a little girl people constantly said to her, "You look just like your daddy." She never responded verbally, but her nonverbal response was always the same. She would drop her head and shoulders and appear hurt. Knowing how much she adored her dad, I couldn't imagine why that bothered her so much. Finally one day someone said it again, and it was the straw that broke the camel's back. She ran to me, buried her face in my chest and cried, "Why do people always say that I look like Daddy?" All of a sudden it dawned on me what the problem was. There was a discrepancy between what the person meant and what Emily heard. She thought being told that she looked like her dad meant she looked masculine. Being a prissy little girl who never could have enough lace sewn on her dress, of course that bothered her.

Putting My Dress-Up Clothes Away

With that realization I quickly said, "Emily, it's that beautiful blond hair and those gorgeous blue eyes that they're talking about."

"Really?" she questioned with great relief, and off she ran. From that time until now she takes great pride when anyone tells her she looks like her dad.

In the creation story, we are told that God made us in His image. Have you ever really thought about what that means? While Emily is the spitting image of her dad, I don't think that's necessarily what the Scripture means when it says we are created in our heavenly Father's image. Let's consider a few possibilities.

Could it mean that we were created to live eternally? Think about it. Plants and animals were not created to live eternally. They live and die and go back into the food chain. We, on the other hand, were born to live forever. We don't even have a choice about that. The only choice we have is *where* we live forever. We can choose to live eternally with God or eternally apart from God. What's your choice?

Could being created in the image of God mean that we were created to think, reason, and make choices? After all, animals don't have that capacity. They live by instinct. If they need something, they go after it. We, on the other hand, were created to look at our needs, wants, and desires and make decisions based on what we think God wants for us and His creation. Our decisions are not based just on what we want but on what's best for other people and the incredible world God created.

Could being created in the image of God mean that He created us with the capacity to reflect His character—to have His mind? What is God's character? When we read about Him in Scripture, we find that He is loving, joyful, patient, kind, gentle, faithful, compassionate, and forgiving—just to name a few.

The apostle Paul told the Philippians to have the mind of Christ. The NIV translation calls it the *attitude* of Christ. Listen to Paul's words. "Your attitude should be the same as that of Christ Jesus: Who, being in very nature God, did not consider equality with God something to be grasped, but made himself nothing, taking the very nature of a servant, being made in human likeness. And being found in appearance as a man, he humbled himself and became obedient to death—even death on a cross!" (Philippians 2:5-8).

Perhaps, then, being created in God's image is not so much that we look like Him but that we can have a relationship with Him. And because we have a relationship with Him, we can behave like Him. That's why Scripture instructs us to "be imitators of God" (Ephesians 5:1).

Let me ask you, do you imitate God? I mean, when people look at you can they say, "She is the spitting image of her Father—her heavenly Father?" I personally believe that's what God had in mind when He created us in His image.

Dear Heavenly Father,
I am so thankful to be Your child. How awesome it is to know that I can have a personal relationship with You. Help me today to allow Your Holy Spirit to produce those qualities in my life so that people can say that I am Christ-like in all that I do. I want to be just like You.

In Jesus' Name,
Amen

Chapter 16

The First Big Blowout

"However, each one of you also must love his wife as he loves himself, and the wife must respect her husband."
—Ephesians 5:33

Scripture Reading
Ephesians 5:22-33

The first big blowout in our marriage was over something as silly as the garbage. The garbage, mind you—worthless, stinking stuff commonly referred to as trash.

Early on the morning of the first big blowout, I pointed to the garbage and said, "There's the garbage," to which Waylon nodded his head. A few hours passed, but nothing happened with the garbage. So I intentionally moved it to the doorway, knowing that Waylon would have to move it in order to get out. What do you suppose he did? Say it, ladies. You know. Did he take the garbage out? Of course not. He stepped *over* the garbage and kept right on going.

Well, by that time I was furious and ready to give him the penance of three days of silence. I considered a week, but the punishment didn't seem to fit the crime so I kept it to three days. To go along with the silent treatment I also planned to show him some serious lips—big-time poked-out lips. I was M-A-D!

When he came back, sensing that the emotional thermometer had dropped below freezing—deathly silence, icy cold nods, and extremely curt yeses or nos—he tried to put his arms around me—kissing up they call it nowadays. That made me even madder! This was no time for that lovey-dovey stuff. Oh, no! And just as he was about to ask me what was the matter, he spied my lips. I had them so poked out it looked like a wasp had stung me. To top it all off, he acted like he was clueless as to why I was so irritated. (Actually, he really was clueless. Waylon is not a very good actor nor does he aspire to be.) So he popped the question, "Martha, what's the matter?"

I glared at him and asked, "What do you mean, what's the matter? Look at that garbage!" You'd have thought he was a literal-minded preschooler because he did exactly as I said. He looked straight at the garbage and then back at me with a puzzled look on his face. Knowing that he just wasn't getting it, I asked him point blank, "Why haven't you taken the garbage out? It's three o'clock in the afternoon, and that stinking garbage has been sitting there all day long!" I thought to myself, "You are a college graduate who is now working on a Master's degree—surely you can figure this one out!"

Then he answered, "Did you want me to take the garbage *out?*" I thought, "I'm in trouble; I'm in trouble. I have married a man who doesn't even know garbage when he sees it." (Isn't it amazing how irrationally we think when we are upset?) Then I said very defensively, "Absolutely!"

Listen to his next line. "Why didn't you say you wanted me to take the garbage out?"

Extremely frustrated and irritated, I thought to myself, "For crying out loud, what on earth do you think I have been asking you to do all day?"

Then it dawned on me—I hadn't actually said anything about taking the trash *out*. I had not asked him one time. Obviously, I was expecting him to read my mind.

Ladies, the reality is our husbands can't read our minds nor do they have any desire to. They are men. They will never be able to view life from a woman's perspective just as we will never be able to see it from their point of view. The truth is that God made us male and female and wired us very differently. Have you noticed?

Some women spend their marriages trying to make their husbands think like a woman. If you are one of those women, my advice to you is—give it up! It ain't gonna happen. More than likely, your husband is never going to see things from your perspective because he is a man. You married your husband because he's a man. Let him be a man. Instead of fretting over your differences, celebrate his uniqueness. Accept that he is "wild at heart" as the John Eldredge book says. That's the way God made him. Remember those wedding vows—for better or for worse, to love, honor, and cherish till death do us part? Then love him. Respect him. Appreciate him. You'll be shocked at what a difference it will make in your relationship.

Father,
I wouldn't take anything for my marriage. I am so blessed. But there are times when conflict erupts simply because we are so different. Forgive me for being stubborn and having unrealistic expectations of my husband. Instead help me to celebrate our differences, appreciating my husband for who You made him to be. Help me to fulfill my marriage vows to love, honor, respect, and appreciate him.

In Jesus' Name,
Amen

Chapter 17

You Want Gucci? No Problem!

"Charm is deceptive, and beauty is fleeting;
but a woman who fears the Lord is to be praised."
—Proverbs 31:30

Scripture Reading
Colossians 3:12-17

Five years ago my daughters and I went on a memorable weekend to New York City. If I told you everything we did in such a short time you wouldn't believe me. Let's just say we made the most of those four days.

Knowing our time was limited, we had everything all mapped out—certain places we wanted to go and Broadway plays we had tickets to see. At the top of the list were Miss Liberty, Central Park, the Empire State Building, and last but not least, Chinatown.

Chinatown is one of those areas in New York where you can buy fake anything—"knock-offs" they call them—fake Rolex watches, fake Oakley sunglasses, and so on. All three of us decided we wanted a purse.

Putting My Dress-Up Clothes Away

With little difficulty Anna and I spied the fake purses that we wanted. Emily, however, had a little problem because the *style* of the purse that she liked did not have the *label* she wanted. She wanted a Gucci, but it was a DKNY. Overhearing Emily's dilemma and determined not to miss a sale, the Vietnamese sales lady quickly interjected, "You want Gucci? No problem!" She yanked that DKNY insignia off the purse so fast that it would make your head spin, quickly pulled out a drawer with a hundred Gucci insignias in it, picked one up, and with two little taps of a hammer changed that once DKNY purse into a Gucci. Off we went, three satisfied customers sporting our new not-Gucci purses and our new not-Oakley sunglasses.

To this day when I carry that knock-off Gucci purse someone will say, "I love your purse." I always chuckle and say, "Thank you. You can get one just like it in New York City—for 15 bucks." I often wonder if they would have liked it if it had a big W for Wal-Mart instead of the big G for Gucci. How sad that we live in a society that is more concerned about the label than what the label is on.

Years ago I worked with a lady who liked a particular outfit I wore from time to time, and told me so, often. Finally, one day when she complimented the outfit I said, "Thank you so much. It came from K-Mart." You know, it was the strangest thing. She never mentioned that outfit again.

It's not only labels that matter so much. For example, can you believe what a difference one to four inches make in ladies' pants? Cropped pants are "in" now, but the same pants would have been "out" and called "high-waters" years ago.

Right after cropped pants became popular, I went to the mall to buy a pair. When I told the saleslady what I was looking for, she said, "Don't you just love cropped pants? They are so fashionable nowadays. I feel so out-of-style in my regular pants." For her it was a self-esteem issue. I remember thinking to myself, "How sad that the length of our pants can determine how we feel about ourselves." I believe with all my heart that God wants us to take care of our bodies and look our best, but I don't think He wants us to determine our worth by our appearance.

Don't get me wrong. I know some beautiful women. There's nothing wrong with being beautiful. The Bible deliberately tells us about several beautiful women—Sarah, Rebekah, and Rachel, to name a few. And we don't know what the Proverbs 31 woman looked like, but her outfits were to die for—fine silk and purple. She was dressed for success!

What is the picture that the Bible paints of being dressed for success? It is found in Colossians 3:12-14, where Paul said, "Clothe yourselves with compassion, kindness, humility, gentleness and patience. Bear with each other and forgive whatever grievances you may have against one another. Forgive as the Lord forgave you. And over all these virtues put on love, which binds them all together in perfect unity."

You see, it doesn't matter whether I am carrying a Gucci purse or wearing cropped pants, but it does matter whether or not I am wearing compassion, kindness, humility, gentleness, and patience—it matters to everyone I meet. No one's life will be better because I carry a Gucci purse or wear cropped pants, but many lives will be affected in a positive way if I clothe myself with godly virtues.

The point I am trying to make is that God wants us to dress for success, but by His standards. So choose your clothes carefully, and by all means, dress for success!

Dear God,
Please help me to dress in a way that is pleasing to You, but more importantly help me to clothe myself with godly virtues that will make everyone's day more pleasant.

In Jesus' Name,
Amen

Chapter 18

A Crying Shame

"Don't be afraid; you are worth more than many sparrows."
—Luke 12:7b

Scripture Reading
Luke 12:6-7

It wasn't the building that caught my eye as I taxied to the Nashville airport. It was the bold capital letters that were affixed to the side of the building: RAPE AND SEXUAL ABUSE CENTER—CHILDREN'S CENTER FOR RAPE AND SEXUAL ABUSE. "What a crying shame," I thought, "for anyone to need such a place." An overwhelming sadness flooded my heart just thinking about all the people who have been victimized and forever scarred by such heartless, heinous crimes. What a paradox for this building to catch my attention in a city known as Music City, USA—a city with countless victims whose lives have no music because they have been sexually violated.

You may be saying, "I have never been abused," or "I don't know anyone who has been abused." Well, if you haven't, stop right now and thank God. Then pray for your friends who have been abused, but you don't know about it. According to the latest statistics, one out of four women has been victimized by some type of sexual crime. That means that you or someone you know *has* been affected. Because sexual abuse victims live with fear of exposure and being misunderstood, they or you suffer in silence—often being destroyed from within by guilt and shame.

It is not uncommon for a woman to say to me with much pain in her voice, "Martha, can we talk sometime? I have something to share with you that I've never shared with anyone else. Can we meet somewhere with some privacy?" I have learned over the years not to speculate, but more times than not it means one of two things—either she will reveal that someone very close to her has chosen a homosexual lifestyle or that she has been sexually abused.

When we meet, she usually begins by asking for complete confidentiality. Then she'll say, "I don't know if I can get the words out. What I'm about to tell you is very painful. It's always on my mind. Hardly a day goes by that I don't think about it." With quivering lips and streaming tears, she'll take a deep breath and try to say what she came to say. But for fear of what I will think or fear that I will tell, she stumbles and fumbles in her attempt to articulate something too painful to say aloud. Her fear is that it will become more real (if that were possible) if she hears herself describe it.

Watching her anguish propels me to say it for her. I might interrupt her and say, "I bet you have been sexually abused, haven't you?" Although she doesn't respond verbally, her body language communicates loud and clear. As lovingly and as sympathetically as I can, I try to dispel any kind of judgmental spirit she has anticipated from me. That's the last thing she needs since many women who have been abused live with an unbearable amount of self-condemnation. How mean and cruel Satan is to make the victim of a sexual crime feel such intense remorse, guilt, and shame because of something she had no control over.

When I was a teenager, a young child was raped in a neighboring town. The evening news spotlighted the story and included an interview with a local pastor. In his feeble attempt to explain why this heinous crime had been committed, he said, "I had a hard time convincing the parents that it was God's will." Can you believe that? Is that the way God is described in the Bible? No it isn't. Instead He is described as "righteous in all his ways and loving toward all he has made" (Psalm 145:17). He is "compassionate and gracious…abounding in love" (Psalm 103:8). He stays "close to the brokenhearted and saves those who are crushed in spirit" (Psalm 34:18). Does that sound like a God who wills for little children or anyone else to be victimized?

Although this incident happened many years ago, I remember it as though it was yesterday. I still cringe at the thought that God could be blamed for such unconscionable behavior.

Let's put the blame where it rightfully belongs. Anytime we choose to use our free will to harm someone else, we are to blame—not God. Unfortunately, we all choose from time to time to make awful decisions that incur devastating consequences. When a person chooses to commit rape or any other sexual crime, that is not God's will. I am certain that it breaks the heart of God for any of His children to experience such an atrocity.

In the sixteenth chapter of Genesis we read about Hagar, a slave woman who was physically and verbally abused by her owner. When she couldn't stand the abuse anymore she ran away into the desert. There God reassured her that He was aware of her plight. Hagar was comforted and gave God the name, "The One who sees me" (Genesis 16:13). Dear sister, do you hear the significance of that name? God wants you to know that while the crime against you was done in secret, it was not hidden from Him. He is still "the One who sees." The Bible says "The eyes of the Lord are everywhere, keeping watch on the wicked and the good" (Proverbs 15:3). He saw the whole thing that happened to you. He hated it then, and He hates it now. What hurts His heart today is that you continue to listen to the voice of the accuser—allowing him to keep you bound in fear and shame by convincing you that you are worthless and useless because you have been abused.

Without a doubt, what has happened to you is awful. But don't confuse who you are with what has happened to you. If you know the Lord, you are His treasured possession—chosen and dearly loved. You see, God's love is not predicated on what has happened to you. God couldn't love you more if you had not been abused, and He doesn't love you any less because you have been abused. (I am indebted to Beth Moore and her Bible studies for enlightening me on this sensitive subject.)

If you have identified with anything I have written today, I want you to know that I have prayed for you—some of you by name, others in general. I have prayed that God will enable you to hear His tender, compassionate voice rather than the accusing voice of Satan who is the father of lies, deception, and shame. I pray that you will allow God to put His loving arms around you and whisper the truth to you. "Are not five sparrows sold for two pennies? Yet not one of them is forgotten by God. Indeed, the very hairs of your head are all numbered. Don't be afraid; you are worth more than many sparrows" (Luke 12:6-7).

Gracious Father,
I know it breaks Your heart every time one of Your children is hurt in any way, especially as the victim of a crime such as sexual abuse. I pray today for anyone reading this devotional who has been violated. Give her the courage to seek help and break the stronghold of silence in which Satan has bound her. Please hold her close today so she can hear Your words of love, compassion, and healing.

In the Loving Name of Jesus,
Amen

Chapter 19

Fiasco in the Ladies' Room

"A time to weep and a time to laugh...."
—Ecclesiastes 3:4

Scripture Reading
Ecclesiastes 3:1-8

Isn't it amazing what we do sometimes when we don't have our minds on what we are doing? Like me, you may have a few stories you aren't necessarily proud of that provide a good laugh for others.

Several years ago I went to a quaint little Victorian restaurant for tea with Emily and a friend. On my way in, I made a quick stop by the ladies' room while Emily and her friend got us a table. I knew it would only be a few minutes before I would join them since the restroom is not a place where you hang out for very long. It's not a place where noteworthy experiences normally happen. However, my stop by the ladies' room that day was very memorable. It was memorable, but not something I wanted to share. Who in their right mind would want to join a tea party and announce: "Hey, y'all. Guess what I just did. I flushed my sunglasses down the toilet!" Not me. My lips were sealed *until* or *if* I chose to disclose my little mishap.

It all happened so fast. When I bent over to flush the toilet, my expensive Oakley sunglasses, which were hooked to the front of my dress, slipped off and fell in. I had no opportunity to intercept them on the way down. I was so aggravated with myself! If those sunglasses had been a cheap pair it wouldn't have been a big deal, but those were *real* Oakleys—my first pair. Initially I thought about trying to retrieve them, but I decided to let those "shades" (as my mother used to call them) go! I hate public restrooms, and I wasn't going to try to fish them out. But then, being Miss Conscience, I began to feel guilty, imagining the tearoom flooded and the poor manager scratching her head wondering what in the world went wrong.

When I snapped back to reality, I knew I had to confess—and fast. "Ma'am," I said to the manager in a very remorseful voice, "I hate to tell you this, but I just flushed my sunglasses down your toilet. I am so sorry." (You won't believe her reply.)

"Did you mean to?" she asked, I guess for lack of a better response.

"Are you crazy?" I thought to myself. "Of course I didn't mean to flush my Oakleys. Do I look that dumb?" but I just said, "No, I didn't," instead.

She immediately started to laugh and said, "Don't worry about it, sweetie. I just appreciate your telling me. Most people wouldn't have bothered."

Again I thought, "And I know why. It's not exactly easy to 'fess up to something so careless and embarrassing when you could've just as easily kept your mouth shut and no one would have ever known."

"It's probably not the first time that's happened," she continued, "and it probably won't be the last."

Thank goodness for nice, empathetic people. I don't know what I expected her to say or do, but I was glad she didn't go ballistic over it. I bet you, if the truth were known, she had done the same thing or something similar. What about you? When I tell this story, you would be surprised at the number of people who come up to me and say, "I can tell you one better than that"—and they do. Believe me, I have heard some funny stories about fiascos in the ladies room, and I am thrilled every time someone tops mine.

I wish I could tell you that those sunglasses were the *only* sunglasses or the only extraneous objects that have made their way into the toilet, but there is one more confession I must make. I also dropped a set of car keys in there, and to top it all off the keys weren't mine. They belonged to my friend. I can definitely say she is a friend because she didn't kill me when I told her that I had a mishap with her keys in the restroom. (Sometime when we have a Frappuccino together I'll fill you in on all the details. It was a fiasco if there ever was one!)

What kind of spiritual application can I possibly make with these ludicrous stories? Choose your friends wisely, and don't let them hold your keys or your sunglasses in the restroom? Or wait to see if the tearoom floods before you 'fess up? No, I think the best application I can draw from this is to remind us to lighten up. Knowing that things are going to happen, both good and bad, we have to make the best of whatever circumstances we find ourselves in. While there are many situations in life that are not funny, much of life is funny if we put it in the proper perspective. There are times when we mess up and the best thing we can do is laugh.

What I did with my sunglasses and keys is the equivalent of flushing a hundred dollar bill down the toilet, but I don't think it's a sin. No, those were honest mistakes—accidents. While I will be the first to admit that carelessness was the culprit, it was not the end of the world.

For years I taught fourth grade, and it broke my heart to see children, little girls especially, fall apart at the slightest provocation. As young as ten years old many of them were already making life miserable for themselves and those around them by making mountains out of molehills. On numerous occasions, I tried to explain to them that life is full of problems—some big and some small—but in order to make it through life we have to know the difference between a real problem and a minor inconvenience or honest mistake. I often told them that if they wasted all their tears on silly stuff, they weren't going to have any tears left when something really big happened. If a student persistently overreacted, I usually resorted to drama. Seeing me react in an unreasonable way helped the class realize that we have options about the way we respond to situations. Most of the time the class wound up in stitches while learning a very valuable lesson about life.

Little girls grow up to be big girls, and I'm afraid some of us have never learned to tell the difference between big stuff and small stuff. I know women who react to a broken fingernail about the same way they do to a sick child. How sad! Wise is the woman who asks God to help her put life in the proper perspective—labeling each situation for what it really is. So lighten up! Don't take yourself so seriously.

There's one more thing. A few Sundays ago I ran into a former Bible Study member who had heard the stories I just shared. And it just so happens that I ran into her in the restroom at church. After a quick hello she said, "I think about you every time I come into the restroom at church." Realizing that what she had just said could be taken the wrong way, she quickly continued, "I mean those funny stories about your keys and sunglasses."

Knowing she didn't mean any harm, I laughingly replied, "What a claim to fame!" After I left the restroom, I thought to myself, "What a great antidote for pride."

Lord,

There are days when things just don't go the way I think they should. In fact, some days just seem to unravel right before my eyes. Help me accept the blame for those things that happen because of my carelessness, but help me not to be too hard on myself when things happen that are beyond my control. Allow me to see the humor in situations that might otherwise make me cry.

In Jesus' Name,
Amen

Chapter 20

Lemons but not Lemonade

"I thank my God every time I remember you."
—Philippians 1:3

Scripture Reading
Philippians 1:1-11

The front of the card said, "If life gives you lemons...." Knowing that it was going to say, "Make lemonade," on the inside, I put it back and continued searching for a card for a friend who was very unhappy with her job. My search, however, proved to be unproductive until for some unknown reason I went back to the lemon card and picked it up again. I reread the front, "If life gives you lemons." Then I opened it and it said, "Stick 'em in your bra—can't hurt, might help!" I burst out laughing right there in the store and exclaimed, "Oh yeah! This one's a keeper. It's absolutely perfect!" With a smile on my face, proud as a peacock, I purchased the card and took it home. I could hardly wait to send it to my friend.

As soon as I got home, I signed it, addressed it, and put it in the mailbox. But afterwards I started worrying that my friend might be offended—I mean the part about her bra needing a little help. So I walked out to the mailbox, got the card, and wrote a disclaimer on the envelope—"Don't take this personally!" Then I returned it to the mailbox. Fortunately the card was a hit! My friend loved it.

A few years later that same friend sent me a card. It was very nice, one she had personalized to make it very special. After reading and enjoying the card, I did something I don't usually do. I turned it over to the back. (No, I wasn't trying to see if it was a Hallmark or how much it cost.) I don't know what possessed me to do such a thing, but boy, was I glad. There was a question on the back of the card that read, "If you were wearing a two-piece bathing suit and had to hide a chicken in it, which piece would you hide it in?" I laughed hysterically wondering if my friend knew that question was on the back of the card. I was dying to find out!

I picked up the phone and called her. When she answered, I quickly thanked her for her thoughtfulness. Then I said, "I think the question on the back of the card is hysterically funny!"

After a few moments of silence, she sheepishly inquired, "What question?"

"You know—the question about the chicken and the two-piece bathing suit," I said with a giggle.

"No, I don't know what you are talking about," she anxiously confessed. Then she added, "You're kidding me, aren't you?"

"No, I'm not kidding. On the back of your card there is a question. Let me read it to you. 'If you were wearing a two-piece bathing suit and had to hide a chicken in it, which part would you hide it in?'" Then I added, "You know I couldn't make up anything that funny!"

I could tell by her silence that she was both perplexed and embarrassed, so I said very reassuringly, "It's nothing to worry about. I think it's a hoot! I just hope I don't ever have to hide a chicken in either piece!"

I still have that card. It brings me almost as much joy today as it did when I first received it.

What is it about a card or a note that means so much? Is it because it demonstrates that someone was thinking about us and cared enough to let us know? I think that's it exactly. When I get the mail, the first thing I do is look to see if there is anything personal—I mean something that looks hand-addressed with my name on it. If there is, I rip the envelope open with great anticipation to see what's written inside and who it's from.

So what's my point? It's to remind us that other people enjoy getting a "pick-me-up" in the mail just like we do. They enjoy getting notes and cards that make them feel all warm and fuzzy on the inside too. You may be protesting that you are not the best card shopper or note writer. Believe me—I understand. I'm not either, but I am amazed at how much my meager efforts seem to mean to others.

My daughters are great card shoppers and note writers. They always seem to find the perfect card for every occasion. However, it's not only the printed message on the card that is so heartwarming. It's those two little personal sentences that they add at the bottom that bring tears to my eyes. After reading their cards, I immediately place them on the windowsill above the kitchen sink as a constant reminder of my daughters' love and affection. After a few weeks, their cards are tucked away in a special box where I keep all my treasures. From time to time when my heart gets heavy or when I'm discouraged, I know where to find an instant dose of encouragement. What a blessing!

Can you imagine what it must have been like for the churches in Corinth, Ephesus, Philippi, and Thessalonica to read over and over again the words of the apostle Paul? He wrote them words of reprimand, yes, but also words of affirmation and expressions of love and appreciation. How thrilling it must have been for the church at Philippi to receive a letter from him that said,

> I thank my God every time I remember you. In all my prayers for all of you, I always pray with joy because of your partnership in the gospel from the first day until now, being confident of this, that he who began a good work in you will carry it on to completion until the day of Christ Jesus. It is right for me to feel this way about all of you, since I have you in my heart; for whether I am in chains or defending and confirming the gospel, all of you share in God's grace with me. God can testify how I long for all of you with the affection of Christ Jesus. —Philippians 1:3-8

Wow! Now that's a keeper! I bet it went into their treasure box too. Well actually, God preserved it in His treasure box, the *Holy Bible*, which contains words of hope, comfort, and love.

Perhaps you have prayed and thanked God today for someone special in your life. That's great. But wouldn't it be even better to let that person know, like the apostle Paul did? Who is it that God is bringing to your mind this very moment? More than likely that is the person God wants you to write today.

Go ahead. Pick up your pen. Make someone's day. Write a note that expresses your heart or find a card that imparts words of encouragement and strength. It may be the very thing that gets that special someone through the day or makes them feel loved and appreciated. I know from personal experience. (And just in case, you might want to read the back of the card. You never know when you might be asking about their swimsuit and a chicken!)

Dear Heavenly Father,
Thank You for Your words of encouragement and wisdom that You give us day by day in the Bible. Thank You also for friends who take the time to write notes and send cards that celebrate the happy times with us and cheer us up when we are down. Help us to remember to do the same for others. Thank You for reminding me today to write a note to _____.

In Jesus' Name,
Amen

Chapter 21

The Peacemaker

"Blessed are the peacemakers, for they will be called sons of God."
—Matthew 5:9

Scripture Reading
James 3:13-18

Peacemaker or troublemaker—which one are you? James would say it all depends on the kind of wisdom you live by. According to him, there are two kinds—earthly wisdom and heavenly wisdom. Earthly wisdom tells you to look out for yourself. It's based on selfishness, which always breeds conflict. Heavenly wisdom, on the other hand, is "first of all pure; then peace-loving, considerate, submissive, full of mercy and good fruit, impartial and sincere" (James 3:17). This kind of wisdom looks out for others. It always seeks to defuse conflict. What it all boils down to is this—earthly wisdom produces troublemakers and heavenly wisdom produces peacemakers.

At the carwash the other day I overheard two senior adults talking.

"How you getting along, John?" one asked.

"I'm doing fine now that I had my peacemaker put in," John replied.

Knowing the elderly gentleman was having a senior moment when he said *peacemaker* instead of *pacemaker*, I chuckled to myself. But then I thought about how awesome it would be if people could actually get a "peacemaker" implanted into their heart—how wonderful it would be if every time they wanted to be unkind, negative, and critical, their "peacemaker" would kick in, take control, and make them kind, loving, and considerate instead. I immediately began to make a list of those, in my opinion, who would qualify for a transplant. "Oh, what a difference it would make in their homes, in their workplaces, and, yes, in their churches," I thought. Going back over my eligibility list, making sure no one was left out, I discovered that I had overlooked one person—me. From time to time I'm the one who needs a peacemaker.

In the Sermon on the Mount Jesus said, "Blessed are the peacemakers, for they will be called sons of God" (Matthew 5:9). "Blessed" means happy, but not "ha ha" kind of happy. Rather, it's that deep sense of satisfaction that comes with knowing you're doing the right thing—living the right way. When we're peacemakers we're living the right way, behaving like the children of God. When we're being troublemakers we aren't. I like the way *The Message* translates this verse: "You're blessed when you can show people how to cooperate instead of compete or fight."

Showing people how to live together peacefully is the right way to live; however, it certainly doesn't come naturally, and it's not necessarily easy. In fact, there are times when fighting and competing are much more natural and easy. They even seem like the right thing to do. That's where we need wisdom—the right kind of wisdom.

Earthly wisdom, unfortunately, is the wisdom of choice for most people. It's the kind of wisdom that allows and sometimes encourages people to misbehave and feel good about it, often motivating them to "stir the pot" in times of conflict instead of being a peacemaker. I was guilty of that very thing today. Instead of letting something go, I had to put my two cents in and "stir the pot," knowing full well that the Holy Spirit was prompting me to do otherwise. I intentionally chose earthly wisdom because it allowed me to say what I wanted to say—the "low road" as my husband calls it. I chose to be a troublemaker. But I didn't have to choose the low road—"the unspiritual and of the devil" road as James calls it (James 3:15). I could just as easily have chosen the "high road"—the one that would have caused me to be a peacemaker.

Back to my original question—troublemaker or peacemaker, which one will you be? It's up to you and will depend on the kind of wisdom you choose. While there's no such device as a "peacemaker" that can be implanted into our hearts, as Christians we can access the power of the Holy Spirit day or night, and He will grant us all the heavenly wisdom we need. James said, "If any of you lacks wisdom, he should ask God, who gives generously to all...." (James 1:5).

Dear Everlasting Father and Prince of Peace,
When I encounter conflict today, help me to access the heavenly wisdom You generously provide. Help me to be a peacemaker through the prompting of the Holy Spirit that You have implanted in my heart.

In Jesus' Name,
Amen

Chapter 22

Dirt in Her Baby's Eyes

"I praise you because I am fearfully and wonderfully made."
—Psalm 139:14a

Scripture Reading
Psalm 139:12-18

Anna was an only child for five and a half years, but she so desperately wanted to be a sister. Knowing the only way that was possible was for us to have a baby, she made her request. Little did she know that we had been trying for two years to have another child.

Finally, in the middle of a career change for my husband (wouldn't you know), I conceived. Anna was so excited! "His name will be David Harrison if it's a boy and Emily if it's a girl," she declared. Anna liked the name David because David Harrison was a sixteen-year-old boy in her carpool that she had a crush on, and Emily because we had recently received two birth announcements—both baby girls named Emily. We didn't know if Anna actually liked the name Emily or if she just assumed

Putting My Dress-Up Clothes Away

all girl babies were named Emily.

As soon as my pregnancy was confirmed and announced, we thought a ride to Baptist Hospital would be a good place to start preparing for the new baby. We knew that no matter how much Anna said she wanted a baby, sharing us with a sibling after having all our love and undivided attention for more than five years would be a big adjustment.

As we drove by the hospital, we told Anna this was the place where the doctor would get her baby sister or baby brother out of her mommy's tummy. I'll never forget her reaction. While sitting quietly in the backseat and listening intently to every word we were saying, she emphatically stated—actually it sounded almost blasphemous, "I sure hope God doesn't get any dirt in my baby's eyes." Bewildered, Waylon and I looked at each other wondering where in the world that statement came from. "You do know," she continued as if to inform us about where babies come from, "that God makes them out of dirt, don't you?" Obviously this little girl had been paying attention to her Sunday School teacher the day they talked about Adam and Eve. I don't know if the rest of the creation story impressed her or not, but the dirt part surely did.

Knowing that getting dirt in the baby's eyes was a serious concern for Anna, we assured her that the doctor would be very careful birthing her new baby. Thankfully, that seemed to satisfy her anxiety. We were relieved that the discussion ended there because you never know where the conversation may lead when you start talking about babies—how they got in their mommy's tummy, exactly how the doctor is going to get them out, and so on. Little did we know that we would spend the next seven months answering those questions, along with several more.

I vividly remember the day we brought Emily home from the hospital. Anna came with Waylon to the hospital to pick us up. She was beside herself with excitement. But that excitement was short-lived and soon turned to disappointment when we got home. After laying Emily in her crib Anna asked, "Is that *all* she does?" Anna didn't make a paragraph out of that sentence, but we felt sure we knew exactly what she meant: "Do you mean to tell me that you have built me up for seven months for this? This baby can't do anything except lie there!" We had no way of knowing what her expectations were—the only thing we could figure out was that Anna thought Emily was going to chase her down the hall as soon as we got home from the hospital. After a few days the excitement resumed, and she enjoyed being the big sister and helping me with the baby.

The birth of a baby is truly a miracle—something that only God can do. When Anna was pregnant with both our grandsons, we couldn't wait each week to receive an update on the baby's development via an email from a website called BabyCenter.com. I'll never forget the week it said that our baby was about the size of a tube of lipstick, and all its vital organs were in place. I was so amazed! I felt like the psalmist when he exclaimed, "Such knowledge is too wonderful for me, too lofty for me to attain" (Psalm 139:6).

Yesterday I took care of my newest grandson, Chase. He is an extremely affectionate baby. Since the day he was born he has loved to be rocked and cuddled. He sleeps if you hold him, and he sleeps if you lay him down, so I just hold him. As I rocked and prayed for him during his hour-long nap, I thought about how God had knitted this baby together in Anna's womb—how he truly is "fearfully and wonderfully made." I also thought about how special he is and how much God loves him.

Rejoice today that you, too, are special to God. You, too, were personally fashioned by Him—you're no cookie cutter job. Instead you have your own unique DNA. Take comfort in knowing that God knows all about you—when you get up and when you go to bed. He knows your thoughts and your words before you ever speak them. He also knows every heartache, pain, disappointment, and joy you will ever experience. He will be with you through every one of them. Nothing can happen to you today that will escape his attention.

Loving Father,
"I praise you because I am fearfully and wonderfully made." Thank You that You know all about me and yet You love me anyway. Help me to rejoice today that I am special and securely wrapped in Your love.

In Jesus' Name,
Amen

Chapter 23

Church, Hawaiian Style

"Praise God in his sanctuary; praise him in his mighty heavens."
—Psalm 150:1

Scripture Reading
Psalm 150

God said to Moses, "Then have them make a sanctuary for me, and I will dwell among them. Make this tabernacle and all its furnishings exactly like the pattern I will show you" (Exodus 25:8-9).

Years later God spoke to David about a similar matter. David, the beloved king of Israel, had built himself a luxurious cedar palace while the Ark of the Covenant, which symbolized God's presence, was outside in a tent. This bothered David. He immediately made plans to build a temple to house the ark and provide a place to worship. However, God had other plans. He had chosen someone else to do the job—David's son, Solomon. God told David, "When your days are over and you rest with your fathers, I will raise up your offspring to succeed you, who will

Putting My Dress-Up Clothes Away

come from your own body, and I will establish his kingdom. He is the one who will build a house for my Name, and I will establish the throne of his kingdom forever" (2 Samuel 7:12-13).

No doubt David was disappointed, but he knew that he must trust God. David knew that he *could* trust God because He had proven His credibility time and time again in David's lifetime. The thoughts of how God had blessed him and his family and the promise of future blessings were overwhelming to David. He responded by saying, "Who am I, O Sovereign LORD, and what is my family that you have brought me this far?…How great you are, O Sovereign LORD! There is no one like you, and there is no God but you, as we have heard with our own ears.… Do as you promised, so that your name will be great forever" (Samuel 7:18b, 22, 25b-26a).

God did as He promised. Solomon succeeded his father, David, and four years later he began the construction process. Solomon sent word to Hiram, king of Tyre, "I intend, therefore, to build a temple for the Name of the LORD my God, as the LORD told my father David.… So give orders that cedars of Lebanon be cut for me. My men will work with yours, and I will pay you for your men whatever wages you set" (1 Kings 5:5-6a).

The king of Tyre was obliged to supply Solomon with cedar logs and provide workers. Although it took over seven years to complete, when it was finished, it was magnificent. The workers used gold, silver, bronze, and cedar to make a house of God unlike any other.

Four hundred years later, Solomon's temple was destroyed by the Babylonians, and the Israelites were taken into exile. The city of Jerusalem and the temple lay in ruin for seventy years. Then God spoke again. People like Zerubbabel felt God's tug on their hearts, so they returned to Jerusalem and reconstructed the temple—a structure not nearly as splendid as Solomon's. However, when Herod the Great came to power in 37 B.C., he renovated it, making it larger and more beautiful than ever before. That structure remained until the Romans demolished it in A.D. 70.

Does God care about buildings? Obviously, He does. Otherwise He wouldn't have allowed so much time, thought, effort, and money to be invested in all the structures we have just talked about. He continues to bless congregations who build buildings, both large and small, in His Name today. However, don't be misled into thinking that God is contained in a building—that the only place you can worship is in a certain type of architecture. God made that crystal clear to me several years ago on our vacation to Hawaii.

Thumbing through the yellow pages on Saturday night, we discovered that "church" for us would be held at the Marriott Hotel in Lahaina, Maui, at 8:00 a.m. on Sunday. That sounded great to us. When we arrived and inquired where the Protestant church service would be held, the concierge told us it would be outside near the beach. The following is what I wrote in my journal after we got back to our hotel:

> We went to church as usual today but not in a usual way—not in a sanctuary with padded pews and stained glass windows. "Church" was beneath the shade of coconut and palm trees on the shore of the aqua waters of the Pacific Ocean. None of the elements that we typically think are necessary for "church" were present—no pews, just white plastic folding chairs. No choir, organ, or piano, only congregational singing beneath the azure sky of the island of Maui. We sang the familiar hymns, "How Great Thou Art" and "Savior Like a Shepherd Lead Us," accompanied by a steel guitar, Hawaiian style. It was awesome!
>
> Although the minister spoke about criticism and admonished us to give it lovingly and sparingly, I sat there contemplating all the beauty surrounding me, realizing that the very place where I was worshipping was nothing more than the tip of a mountain protruding out of the bottomless Pacific Ocean.
>
> God reminded me that it's not the place that's necessarily important to Him. What matters is if we really worship Him. He wants us to do more than just show up; God wants us to worship, praise, and glorify Him

whether it's in the confines of a beautiful sanctuary or under the shade of a coconut tree on an island in the middle of the Pacific Ocean.

Dear God,

How awesome You are! How worthy You are to be praised! Help us remember that we can worship, praise, and glorify You wherever we are. We thank You for the buildings that You have provided for us to worship in, but help us never to think that Your glory could ever be confined in any building. Let our churches be special only because they create an atmosphere where we can commune with You.

In Jesus' Name,
Amen

Chapter 24

Can I Just Write Her Off?

"If it is possible, as far as it depends on you,
live at peace with everyone."
—Romans 12:18

Scripture Reading
Matthew 18:15-20

"I don't know what to do," she sobbed over the phone. "I have asked and asked what's wrong, and all she'll say is, 'Nothing.' But I know something is wrong because of the way she's treating me."

"I'm so sorry," I replied sympathetically. "I know what that feels like."

"But I thought she was my friend! If this was someone I had a casual relationship with it wouldn't hurt so bad," she continued. "The worst part is that I can't get her off my mind. Why does our relationship matter so

Putting My Dress-Up Clothes Away

much to me when she doesn't seem to care about it? I have stood by her during some tough times, and is this all I get for it? I've made several attempts to work this problem out—whatever it is—and every time I hit a brick wall. When she says, 'Nothing,' I know that she's not leveling with me. I've told her that I'm sorry if I offended her, but she always says I haven't. This whole thing stinks!"

"It sure does," I said, feeling her pain.

"What am I supposed to do now, Martha, just write her off? That's what I want to do."

"No, I don't think that's what you should do, but you have to find a way to deal with it if she's not going to cooperate."

"Why can't I just forget about her if she doesn't want to be my friend?"

"I don't know, Lauren. Do you think God won't let you give up on your friend?" I asked, trying to sort all of this out myself lest I escalate the problem instead of helping her resolve it.

"I don't know. I have prayed and prayed and prayed. I've even asked God if this is what you get when you invest your life in someone," she said, attempting to defend herself. "If it is, then I'm going to be more selective about my friends. I always thought she loved and respected me, but now I seem to be the object of her anger. I am so confused!"

"Lauren, I'm so sorry. I know this is hard for you. Do you suppose your friend is having some personal problems that you don't know about? I read a book years ago titled, *Why We Act That Way*, and it said that if we could only know what's going on in a person's personal life we might understand them better. Don't misunderstand me. I'm not taking up for your friend, but sometimes it helps to accept and handle the pain our friends inflict upon us if we feel like there is a legitimate reason."

"I don't know of anything. In the past I have been her confidante. She has shared some pretty serious stuff with me about her past, especially her young adult years."

"Hmm," I said, trying to give myself some processing time and time for the Holy Spirit to give me godly insight and wisdom. "When you have prayed about this, do you sense God leading you in any way?"

"No. The thing that I keep going over and over in my mind is that I've done my part. It's up to her. I don't want to open myself up for further hurt. I have written a note, taken her to lunch, called her on the phone, and tried to talk. I have remained warm and friendly. She hasn't. It's not my problem. It's hers. I'm pretty sick and tired of this whole situation!"

"Lauren, I know that sometimes God seems to be silent on issues, but have you stopped to consider that those thoughts you just verbalized didn't come from God?" I asked, trying to get her to realize that there might be another voice she was hearing.

"Oh my goodness. I've never thought about that! But don't you think that I've done my part?" she asked, half apologetically and half defensively.

"Yes, I do think you've done your part, but I don't believe the Bible gives us permission to write people off. While you certainly can't have a relationship with someone who doesn't want one, I think we need to see what the Bible tells us to do in a situation like this," I said, trying not to sound too preachy.

"What does it say?" she asked, genuinely wanting to know. "I have my Bible right here."

"Look up Matthew 18:15-20 and read it to yourself. Then we'll discuss it."

"Okay." After reading the passage she said, "I have done everything it says here except tell it to the church. I have even gotten another friend involved, but it hasn't done any good."

"Look at the latter part of verse 17. Do you see where it says, 'treat him as you would a pagan or a tax collector'?"

"Yes, but I don't know what that means. Can you explain it to me?"

"I'll try. For years that verse didn't make much sense to me either, but then one day it dawned on me that it was saying to treat that person like you would treat someone who is lost. That means you pray for them to turn to God and let Him direct their life. If you read further it says, 'Whatever you bind on earth will be bound in heaven, and whatever you loose on earth will be loosed in heaven.'"

"Okay, just put it in plain English so I can understand. All that is a little confusing to me."

"Here's the deal—broken relationships don't go unnoticed by God. They bother Him. It hurts our Father when two of His children can't get along. He wants us to take the initiative to restore the relationship even if we don't think it's our fault—even if we have tried before. I realize more than likely that's not what you wanted me to tell you when you called this morning, is it?"

"No, it isn't," she said, honestly but not unappreciatively.

"Perhaps the reason you thought you called this morning was for me to give you permission to write your friend off, but it may have been God's way to get you to listen to Him concerning this relationship. What do you think?" I asked, "I believe you have genuinely tried to restore this broken relationship."

"You're probably right," she replied, sounding more at peace than she had throughout the whole conversation. "I think I can see what to do now. I'll just continue to pray for her and wait for God to soften her heart. I know this is not my fault. In my heart I know that I've done everything I should've done except to pray diligently for her. Thank you so much for talking to me this morning. I appreciate it so much."

"I know you do. I'm glad I could help. Now get busy and get your mind on something else. Let God do His work," I said once again, knowing that the Bible truly is "A lamp to my feet and a light for my path" (Psalm 119:105). Thanking God in my heart, I asked, "Would you like to pray for your friend before we get off the phone?"

"That would be great," she said.

Do you have a broken relationship that needs attention? If so, you know what you need to do. Pick up the phone, make a visit, write a letter, pray—whatever is necessary. "For whatever you bind on earth will be bound in heaven, and whatever you loose on earth will be loosed in heaven" (Matthew 18:18).

Lord,
It hurts so bad to be at odds with a friend especially when we know it's not our fault. It hurts even more when we try to reconcile and meet resistance. Thank You for prompting us and giving us courage in situations like I've just described. I know that You want us to live at peace with everyone, especially with our sisters in Christ.

In Jesus' Name,
Amen

Chapter 25

The Mystery of the Lost Purse

"I tell you that in the same way there will be more rejoicing in heaven over one sinner who repents than over ninety-nine righteous persons who do not need to repent."
—Luke 15:7

Scripture Reading
Luke 15:1-31

"Where is it? I know it's out here somewhere. It just *has* to be," I racked my brain as I frantically walked up and down the street looking for my purse. It wasn't that it had a significant amount of money in it. No, it had something much more valuable. It had my identity in it. That's serious! That's why I *had* to find it.

Have you ever lost something of great value that you were desperate to find? My purse was of great value to me. And I had to find it. Something inside compelled me to keep looking. I didn't know if I was trying to think positively or if the Holy Spirit was prompting me to persevere. Let me tell you about it, and see if you can relate.

It all began on a Thursday morning when I hurriedly dashed out of the house on my way to an appointment. Since it was near lunchtime, I decided to swing by a fast food restaurant to grab a bite to eat. It was there I discovered that my purse was missing. I assumed I had left it at home, and it didn't worry me too much initially. A quick call home determined that was not the case. Realizing that time was not on my side, I knew I had to get home—and fast! The clock was ticking!

There was one little problem. With no purse, I didn't have a driver's license. In case I got stopped by the police, I rehearsed a few lines that any decent officer would find sympathetic. I knew a few tears might even come in handy. I don't mean an Academy Award performance—just a little drama.

A thorough search of the house confirmed that my purse was not there, which led to only one conclusion—I had laid it on the trunk of the car while I locked the door and then had driven off with it still on the trunk. Then I had an ingenious idea. I would simulate what I had done earlier that morning to see how long the purse could have stayed on the trunk before it fell off. This was going to be an experiment—a test—one like NASA does before a shuttle launch.

Picture it. First, I went inside and got a gift bag about the size of my purse and filled it with magazines to make it about the same weight as my purse. Then I placed the bag on the trunk of the car and backed out of the garage just as I had done earlier that morning. Looking in the rearview mirror I could see the bag had not budged. It was exactly where I had placed it—so far, so good.

The second phase of the experiment went well too. The bag stayed securely on the trunk down my 100-foot driveway. Phase three was the part of the experiment that revealed where I might have lost my purse. When I turned out of the driveway onto the street, the gift bag slid off the trunk, dumping its contents in the middle of the street.

"Oh my, that's not good!" I thought. Somehow this scientific experiment did not make me feel better—it made me feel worse. It confirmed what I had feared all along—that my purse had fallen off the trunk right in front of my house, and the thief that picked it up hadn't bothered to ring my doorbell and return my purse. I was furious!

Although the experiment indicated that I should cancel credit cards ASAP and secure a new driver's license, I could not let it go. Instead, I walked up and down the street scrutinizing every inch. The neighbors must have thought I was crazy, but I didn't care. I felt compelled to continue the search.

The next day after all the credit cards had been canceled and a new license secured, I said to my husband, "Do you think it would be a good idea if I walked down the street just one more time and looked for my purse?"

Waylon knew that if there had ever been a "yes, dear" moment, this was it. "Sure," he said as he rolled his eyes in disbelief. So off I went on my final mission to solve the mystery of the lost purse.

I searched for about a half mile. No purse. With every step, hope was fleeting. With the river up ahead, I knew no purse on the trunk of any car could survive the jolt it would take going up the incline to the bridge. At that point I prayed, "Lord, if I don't find my purse in the next twelve feet (how about that for being specific in prayer?), I will have to accept the fact that my purse cannot be found or that someone has stolen it." Just as I finished the last phrase, I glanced down an eight-foot embankment, and there was my purse—dangling from a twig, sopping wet from the torrential rain the night before. Initially all I could do was stare in disbelief. Then I began to cry, "Thank You, Lord; thank You for encouraging me to keep looking until I found it! You know how valuable it is to me."

Jesus told three stories in the Gospel of Luke about three people who had lost something valuable to them that they *had* to find. One lost a sheep. One lost a coin. The other lost a son. Jesus described each individual as someone who wasn't willing to stop at anything until he found what he lost.

Do you know what prompted Jesus to tell these stories? He wanted the crowd to understand that all people are valuable to Him, including those society has thrown away and labeled as worthless. He was counteracting criticism that had been made against Him. The religious leaders couldn't understand why Jesus would waste his time talking to social outcasts—people of no value in their eyes. Their attitude was precisely the reason Jesus told these stories. Jesus' implied question was very simple—if a shepherd would care enough to leave ninety-nine sheep to go look for one that was lost, a woman would turn the house upside down searching for one coin that was lost, and a father would wait patiently for a wayward son to come home, why wouldn't Jesus take the time to interact with people who were spiritually lost—eternally lost?

Think for a minute about the people you see when you are out and about—the woman at the laundry, the secretary at your child's school, your next-door neighbor, or someone you do business with who has a questionable reputation. All of these people are valuable to Jesus. But do they know it? Better yet, do they know Jesus? If not, they are lost—just like my purse dangling from the twig. And unless you intentionally take the time to pursue them and talk with them about eternity, they may be lost forever. Would you deliberately take the time today to see someone through the eyes of eternity?

Jesus concluded that every time a person comes to faith in Him there is a party in heaven. He said, "I tell you, there is rejoicing in the presence of the angels of God over one sinner who repents" (Luke 15:10).

Father,

Thank You that You are a God who values each one of us. Help us value the people we see today no matter who they are, what they look like, or what they have done. Help us pursue them as if we lost something of great value so that they can live eternally with You.

In Jesus' Name,
Amen

Chapter 26

Watermelon Coin

"God loves a cheerful giver."
—2 Corinthians 9:7b

Scripture Reading
Acts 5:1-11

There's nothing like trying to worship while wrestling with a preschooler. For those of you who have a three-year-old trying to adjust to "big church," today's thoughts are for you. If you are one of those fortunate moms whose children sleep all the way through church, stop right now and thank God. You don't realize how blessed you are.

When my children were small, I had a friend whose boys slept through every service, day or night. I often wondered how church could have such a sedative effect on her boys while it seemed to stimulate our daughters. Sometimes as I struggled with our girls, I had the urge to pinch one of her boys and wake them up just so she would know what it was like to wrestle during church like the rest of us. I never did that, of course, but it wasn't because I didn't want to.

One Sunday during the worship service all the children, including our three-year-old Emily, went forward for a children's sermon—you know, the kind that the adults get more out of than the children. Someone in the congregation had been to Guatemala on a mission trip and had brought back coins for all the children. The minister talked about missions for a few minutes and then said, "Today, boys and girls, I am going to give each one of you a Guatemalan coin that you can keep." So all the children eagerly reached into the bag, got a coin, and proudly returned to their parents.

The offertory immediately followed the children's sermon. After the amen of the offertory prayer, I gave Emily a quarter to put into the offering plate. As we waited for the plate to pass by, Emily held her quarter tightly in her right hand and her Guatemalan coin in her left hand. However, when the offering plate came to us, she got her hands mixed up and by mistake she put her Guatemalan coin in the plate instead of her quarter. As soon as she did it a look of horror came over her face, and she screamed, I mean *screamed*, "Hey, wait a minute! I want my watermelon coin back!" What did the ushers do? They did exactly what Emily told them to do. They passed the plate back to her. She dug through the offering until she found her "watermelon" coin which she gladly exchanged for her quarter. It was one of those moments that everyone else loves and thinks is so cute but can be a little embarrassing for parents. For days later we talked about our "watermelon" coins.

"God loves a cheerful giver" (2 Corinthians 9:7b). That's what the Bible says. What does it mean? It means God smiles when we give because we want to give. When God sees that we are grateful for the blessings He has given us and that we want to give some of it back to Him, He is happy.

There's a story in the Book of Acts about a couple named Ananias and Sapphira. They were not cheerful givers. They did not make God happy.

They conspired to sell a piece of land and give *part* of the money they had received to the apostles under the pretense that they were giving *all* that they received for the property. Peter, however, could see through their conspiracy and reprimanded them by saying, "Ananias, how is it that Satan has so filled your heart that you have lied to the Holy Spirit and have kept for yourself some of the money you received for the land?...What made you think of doing such a thing? You have not lied to men but to God" (Acts 5:3-4).

This story has a very sad ending. God judged both Ananias and Sapphira. They died on the spot. Their death didn't go unnoticed by the early Christians either. "Great fear seized the whole church and all who heard about these events," according to the writer of Acts (5:11).

Giving is very serious business to God. In the Malachi 3:8-9, God posed a very poignant question to the people of Israel. "Will a man rob God?"

When they asked how they had robbed Him, He said, "In tithes and offerings. You are under a curse—the whole nation of you—because you are robbing me." I suppose they saw giving as an option, like many do today.

Quite often we don't take God seriously when He tells us that He wants us to give our tithe to Him and that He likes it when we give with a cheerful heart. Let me ask you—how do you view giving? Do you see it as a duty? Is it a chore? Do you do it out of fear? Do you resent having to give? Do you do it grudgingly? If you answered yes to any of those questions, you need to take a closer look at who God is and what He expects.

God makes it clear that it's not only the gift that counts, but it's the attitude with which we give it. Paul said it this way, "Whoever sows sparingly will also reap sparingly, and whoever sows generously will also reap generously. Each man should give what he has decided in his heart to give, not reluctantly or under compulsion, for God loves a cheerful giver.... This service that you perform is not only supplying the needs of God's people but is also overflowing in many expressions of thanks to God" (2 Corinthians 9:6-7, 12).

Are you giving sparingly or generously? Are you giving reluctantly or willingly? Without a doubt, it makes God happy when we give because we acknowledge and appreciate all that He has given to us.

Dear God,
You have given me more than I could have ever dreamed. Thank You so much. I know that everything I own really belongs to You. Help me to always remember to be a good steward, to give willingly and generously and with a cheerful heart.

In Jesus' Name,
Amen

Chapter 27

Turn the Light Back On

"Do not let the sun go down while you are still angry."
—Ephesians 4:26b

Scripture Reading
Ephesians 4:26, 29–5:2, 33

Communicate! Communicate! Communicate!—that's the number one rule in marriage. Waylon and I have been married thirty-six years. You'd think by this time we would have worked everything out, seeing eye to eye on most things. It's funny that we know each other so well that we can often finish each other's sentences and yet, like most couples, we still have work to do in the area of communication.

The good news is we can learn to communicate more effectively, but we must be intentional about it. Good communication skills are not acquired by accident. They are learned and must be practiced. What it all boils down to is this—learning to communicate effectively is a lifelong process.

There are many factors involved in communication besides the obvious ones like word choice, listening, and eye contact. Three other biggies should be added to the list—tone of voice, fatigue, and time pressure. Think about it for a minute. Analyze the last time you and your husband had an argument. I can almost guarantee that it was associated with one of these factors—if not all three.

Often we begin our day all stressed out because we are not prepared for the day. We get up late, can't find our clothes, the milk is sour, there's no bread for toast, and the car is on empty. Then, moving at warp speed, we jet off to work. When the workday is over, we rush home totally exhausted. No wonder our tone of voice is not friendly and engaging.

One day Waylon came home from work, and things started off on the wrong foot immediately. He fired at me, and I quickly returned fire. After a few rounds, he looked at me and said, "Can I go out and come back in again?" That's exactly what he did. When he came back in his voice was different. My voice was different. It was amazing what an impact that had on our evening, especially after he relaxed a few minutes and ate supper.

Both spouses need to learn to say, "I'm tired," "I'm stressed," and yes, "I'm hungry." I think you would be amazed at the impact those three little statements could have on a relationship.

What does the Bible say about how spouses should communicate? Actually, it doesn't say a lot specifically about communicating with spouses, but it says a lot about how Christians should communicate with one another. Isn't it interesting that often we read and apply God's Word to other relationships but fail to apply it to the most intimate of all relationships—our marriage?

Jesus told us that our words come out of our hearts (Matthew 12:34). Therefore, if we are having conflict in our marriage due to poor communication, perhaps we should examine our hearts, allowing God to expose any area that is not consistent with His will. If we discover a problem with our tongue, with our ears, or with our body language we need to heed His words of counsel.

Paul told the Ephesians, "In your anger do not sin. Do not let the sun go down while you are still angry." How many nights have you gone to bed angry with your husband? Early in our marriage that happened more times than I would like to admit, and most of the time it was my fault. Waylon is a much more forgiving person than I am. There were times he would have reconciled, but I stubbornly refused. I had a heart problem. It wasn't that I didn't know what the Bible said about being that way, either. I knew the verses well that said, "Reckless words pierce like a sword, but the tongue of the wise brings healing" (Proverbs 12:18), and "A gentle answer turns away wrath, but a harsh word stirs up anger" (Proverbs 15:1).

Many years into our marriage, however, God showed Waylon a very practical way to deal with unresolved conflict at bedtime. If we were still arguing or giving each other the silent treatment after we went to bed, Waylon turned the light back on until we could get the problem resolved. We discovered that it wasn't as easy to say mean, cutting words in the light as it was in the dark. Since that time I can't tell you that we have resolved every conflict before going to sleep, but I can tell you that turning the light back on has made a tremendous difference. Try it and see for yourself.

James 1:19-20 sums it up well when it says, "My dear brothers, take note of this: Everyone should be quick to listen, slow to speak and slow to become angry, for man's anger does not bring about the righteous life that God desires." Quick to listen, slow to speak, and slow to become angry—now that's great advice for any relationship, especially a marriage. God wants us to have marriages that thrive. The only way that is going to happen is if we learn to communicate using the principles found in His Word.

Father,

Our busy lives often bring stress in our marriages. Help us to quickly detect when our hearts are not pure and when we are violating the principles in Your Word. Please give us marriages that thrive, not ones that just merely survive.

In Jesus' Name,
Amen

Chapter 28

Flip-Flops and God's Name

"Thou shalt not take the name of the Lord thy God in vain."
—Exodus 20:7a (KJV)

Scripture Reading
Exodus 20:1-17

Yesterday we were shopping for flip-flops at a souvenir shop at the beach when a four-year-old and her dad walked in. Obviously they were flip-flop shopping too, because as soon as the little girl spied a pair she liked she exclaimed, "Oh my God, look Daddy!" Cringing at the sound of those words my heart sank as I wondered why a four-year-old would say something like that.

The more I thought about it the more my heart hurt because I knew that she was not intentionally taking God's name in vain. I'm certain she didn't have a clue she was saying anything inappropriate. More than likely she was just using an expression she hears at home every day—an expression that she had been *taught* to say by example.

What does the Bible say about taking the Lord's name in vain? The King James Version says, "Thou shalt not take the name of the Lord thy God in vain." The New American Standard Version translates the word *vain* as *misuse*. So back to my question about what the Bible says about taking the Lord's name in vain—it's quite simple—it says don't do it. Period. Yet if we were to carry a pencil and paper around with us today and tally each time we heard His name misused, I think we would be astounded at the results. People often use it without even thinking about what they are saying or whom it represents—the epitome of what it means to take God's name in vain. The little girl gives us a perfect example. She trivialized God's name by using it to express delight over finding a cheap pair of flip-flops and never thought about God at all. Using His name like that makes it insignificant and meaningless, clearly a violation of the third commandment.

The most common way we think about taking the Lord's name in vain is in profanity. I'm certain that vulgar, crude speech is never pleasing to God, but when His name is attached to it, that must hurt His heart. It's like dragging His name through the mud. How disrespectful of us to scream out His name in anger, frustration, or even excitement like the little girl with her flip-flops.

Many Christians become quite smug when taking an inventory of how well they are keeping the Ten Commandments. They look at Number Three and say with pride, "I'm not guilty of taking the Lord's name in vain because I don't curse or use it as an expletive." But could taking the Lord's name in vain refer to more than just what we say? Could it also refer to the way we live? Does calling ourselves Christians while living by the same standards as nonbelievers make God's name seem meaningless, ineffective, and insignificant? When our co-workers observe our work ethic and the way we treat them, does it make them think less of God? If so, that's serious because we are misrepresenting who God is. It is irreverent and irresponsible. It's a sin—one that God does not take lightly.

Have you read the rest of the verse that contains commandment number three? Listen to it. "For the LORD will not hold anyone guiltless who misuses his name" (Exodus 20:7b). That means it matters to God every time we trivialize His name whether it is by crude, vulgar, or inappropriate speech or by an irresponsible lifestyle.

Is the Holy Spirit convicting you of an area where you misuse, trivialize, or discount the Lord's name? Take a few moments and allow Him to expose those areas. Confess them and ask God to help you be more responsible with the way you use His name and the way you represent Him by your lifestyle.

Heavenly Father,
You taught us to pray, "Our Father who art in heaven, hallowed be thy name," but often we never stop to consider what it really means. I admit that I have felt rather smug at times because I don't use profanity and have even been judgmental of those who do. However, today You have reminded me that taking Your Name in vain encompasses so much more than just vulgar speech. Help me to live my life in a way that would never dishonor Your Name. Instead, help me to glorify, exalt, and praise Your Name in all that I do.

In Jesus' Name,
Amen

Chapter 29

The Big Birthday Party

"With praise and thanksgiving they sang to the Lord."
—Ezra 3:11a

Scripture Reading
Ezra 3:7–13

The celebration had been postponed from February until May in hopes of better weather. Our church would be celebrating a big birthday—its 100th, to be exact. The committee planned for months to make this event special for the entire congregation. Wanting an atmosphere of "one big happy family," they planned for us to have one worship service where normally we have three. They were anticipating a crowd of close to 2,000, knowing that some of those who attended would have to worship in the fellowship hall via video on big screens. But that didn't discourage the committee. They had a job to do and intended to do it well.

And well they did. When I returned home after the celebration my heart was filled with such a feeling of gratitude to be a part of what God is doing at First Baptist Church, Covington, Louisiana. We had an electrifying worship experience. It was awesome! There was definitely a sweet, sweet spirit, and we left knowing that we had been in the presence of the living God. It was one of those Transfiguration moments like the one when Peter said to Jesus, "How about we all just stay here—you, Moses, Elijah, James, John, and me" (Matthew 17:1-8). Or perhaps a Mt. Sinai moment like when Moses' face glowed after being in the presence of the Almighty God (Exodus 34:29).

After every song or instrumental piece the congregation broke out into spontaneous applause. Jake, who was two-and-a-half years old at that time, was sitting with his parents beside me, and as the congregation applauded he clapped his little hands and yelled, "Yea! Yea!" I must admit I got a little nervous, though, being afraid he was going to add, "Yea, two points! I love this game!" He and I play basketball together, and that's what we say after each basket. Except for the night we took him to a Hornets game in New Orleans, I don't think Jake had ever been to any kind of activity where there was that kind of excitement and applause. How incredible that he would associate the atmosphere of a basketball game with the atmosphere at church!

While Jake was too young to understand what that day was all about, he knew that church was exciting and a fun place to be. I hope he feels that way for the rest of his life. I hope he never looks at church as humdrum or a meaningless ritual that has to be endured. Instead I hope he sees every Sunday as a celebration of God's power, majesty, and providential love and care.

Our celebration reminded me of Scripture from the Book of Ezra when the Israelites returned from exile to rebuild the temple.

> When the builders laid the foundation of the temple of the Lord, the priests in their vestments and with trumpets, and the Levites (the sons of Asaph) with cymbals, took their places to praise the Lord, as prescribed by

David king of Israel. With praise and thanksgiving they sang to the Lord: "He is good; his love to Israel endures forever." And all the people gave a great shout of praise to the Lord, because the foundation of the house of the Lord was laid. But many of the older priests and Levites and family heads, who had seen the former temple, wept aloud when they saw the foundation of this temple being laid, while many others shouted for joy. No one could distinguish the sound of the shouts of joy from the sound of weeping because the people made so much noise. And the sound was heard far away.
—Ezra 3:10-13

While we didn't lay a foundation or dedicate a new building that day, all of us were keenly aware that anything we have done or will do in the future is because of the foundation that has already been laid for us over the past 100 years by those the writer of Hebrews describes as a "great cloud of witnesses" (Hebrews 12:1). I believe all those many wonderful Christians who have been a part of this great church over the past century were cheering us on. Now our job is to get rid of anything that distracts us or causes us to stumble in our walk with the Lord and build aggressively on the foundation laid for us. Our job as a church is to focus on Jesus and make Him the center and the reason for everything we do as individuals and as a church.

Let me ask you, what is going to church like for you? Do you go there each week expecting nothing to happen in your life, or do you go there expecting to clap your hands and exclaim, "Yea, Yea!" like Jake? Could it be that little Jake's reaction to and participation in the 100th anniversary celebration was much closer to God's definition of what true worship is all about?

Father,
I thank You for instituting the church as a place where I can gather with other believers to sing praises to Your name, pray, and hear Your Word proclaimed.

Help me to never take that for granted or be guilty of just going through the motions. Instead help me to experience the excitement of Jake as I worship You.

In Jesus' Name,
Amen

Chapter 30

My Little Angel

"May the words of my mouth and the meditation of my heart be pleasing in your sight, O Lord, my Rock and my Redeemer."
—Psalm 19:14

Scripture Reading
James 3:2-12

Have you ever said something and then regretted it the minute you got it out of your mouth? I think we all know that feeling. Have you ever started to say something, but a little voice inside you warned, "Don't say it," and then you said it anyway? Perhaps we've all been there, too—many more times than we would like to admit.

Several years ago, I was in a Christmas musical. I don't remember my role, but there was one person's role I will never forget. Actually, he had two roles. In the first scene he was a shepherd, and in the last scene he was an angel. But it wasn't his performance that was so unforgettable. It was an incident that happened offstage the night of the dress rehearsal.

Those of us who had finished our appearance in scene one were goofing off and killing time until we were due back onstage. My shepherd friend joined us after putting on his angel costume for the next scene. As soon as I saw him I thought, "Look at him. Isn't that just like a man? Instead of taking his shepherd costume off, he has rolled it up around his middle and put the angel costume on top of it." Normally I wouldn't have dared address such an issue, but for some unknown reason I proceeded to set—let's just call him Gabriel—straight. "Gabriel," I said, "You need to take that shepherd costume off," as I pointed to the bulge around his middle. Much to my chagrin and without a moment's hesitation he replied with a big grin, "Martha, I don't have my shepherd costume on." Pointing to his middle and laughing uncontrollably he said, "That is all me!" (I don't think I've ever had a mental image of an angel doing a belly laugh, but believe me, I have one now.)

Talk about embarrassing—I wanted to die on the spot! It was one of those Southwest Airlines "Do you wanna get away?" moments. What I would have given for a delete button to forever erase that statement. But, as you know, life has no delete or rewind button. Whatever is said is said. Period. Words can't be erased nor can they be taken back. While I could have kicked myself for making such a thoughtless statement, all the wishing in the world wasn't going to undo what I had said.

Attempting to rescue me, my shepherd/angel friend said, "My wife has been telling me that I need to go on a diet." The only redeeming thing about the whole situation was that my friend thought it was incredibly funny—and he still does, thank goodness.

Quite often our tongue gets us into a heap of trouble. That's probably why the Bible has so much to say about it. In the Book of James, the author talks about things that are small yet powerful. First, he mentions a bit in a horse's mouth. Small yet powerful. Next he mentions a rudder on a ship. Small yet powerful. Finally, he mentions a spark in a forest. Again, small yet powerful. His point is this—the tongue is also a small part of the body, but don't let it fool you. It too is small yet powerful. Just as the bit, rudder, and spark can impact a horse, a ship, and a forest, so can our tongue greatly impact our lives. In fact, our tongue, according to James 3:6b, 8b, "corrupts the whole person, sets the whole course of his life on fire.… It is a restless evil, full of deadly poison."

Proverbs 18:21, paraphrased in *The Message*, warns us, "Words kill, words give life; they're either poison or fruit—you choose." Don't miss the last two words—*you choose*. Make no mistake: we choose how we use our tongue. I heard someone refer to another person as "Machete Mouth" because she tends to have a sharp tongue from time to time. Occasionally I hear someone say, "I just say what I think." How absurd! How dangerous! How ungodly! Some things don't need to be said—even if they are true. Proverbs 29:20 hits the nail on the head when it says, "Do you see a man who speaks in haste? There is more hope for a fool than for him." Let us choose our words with extreme caution and sensitivity to the leadership of the Holy Spirit. God wants our words to be fruit, not poison.

Writing to Christians, James said that there is a grave contradiction when we praise God one minute and rip our brothers and sisters to shreds the next. He said that just as we don't expect fresh water and salt water to come from the same source, neither should words of praise and cursing come from the same mouth. Furthermore, James added that vacillating from words of praise to words that curse is a direct violation of the two greatest commandments: love God and love people.

Years ago I had a precious friend in her eighties. She was a wonderful mother and loved to talk about her family. On one occasion she shared a story about her two sons when they were young. I have never forgotten it. She said one day the phone rang while she was ironing. It was a friend, and before she knew it, she was involved in a rather lengthy conversation, not realizing that her two small boys were paying attention. When she got off the phone, one of them said to her, "Mama, why don't you talk to us as sweet as you talk to the people on the phone?" My, my! Can you imagine how that must have stung? And from a child? Sometimes children are brutally honest. They tell it like it is. Knowing my friend, it probably wasn't that she had said anything unkind, but her boys were just saying, "We'd like for you to use some of that sweet talk with us too."

Often we don't realize how we sound. We are wise when we take into consideration not only the words we use but the tone of voice we use as well. My friend learned a valuable lesson that day. Are you taking note?

Let's look closely at two poignant warnings from Jesus about our tongue. First, Jesus said that what we often label as a problem with our tongue is actually a much more serious, deep-seated problem. It's a heart problem. He said, "For out of the overflow of the heart the mouth speaks. The good man brings good things out of the good stored up in him, and the evil man brings evil things out of the evil stored up in him" (Matthew 12:34b-35). If that's the case, the place to begin when we are trying to improve our speech is not with our words, but with a closer examination of our hearts. We need to ask ourselves, "Do I really have a heart for God?" James 1:26 teaches us that if we consider ourselves religious and yet don't watch what we say, we might need to rethink our religion.

Second, Jesus warned us that we are going to be held accountable for everything we say. "But I tell you that men will have to give account on the day of judgment for every careless word they have spoken. For by your words you will be acquitted, and by your words you will be condemned" (Matthew 12:36-37). Does it strike terror in your heart to know that when you stand before the Lord face-to-face you are going to be ashamed of some of your words?

Today you will speak thousands of words. Choose them carefully. They carry a powerful punch that can bless or destroy. Remember, it's your words that determine the course of your life, and the lives of those around you.

Father,
I pray that You will cleanse my heart and help me to be very careful with the words I speak today. Help me to choose them wisely, knowing that You are holding me accountable for every one of them. Remind me to bless those I see today.

In Jesus' Name,
Amen

Chapter 31

Burning Coals on Her Head

"Do not be overcome by evil, but overcome evil with good."
—Romans 12:21

Scripture Reading
Romans 12:17-21

It was mean. It was unkind. It was untrue. It was an out-and-out lie! It made me so angry I thought I would die! Although many years have passed since she uttered those unkind remarks, the memory of them still hurts. She didn't say it about me. She said it about someone I love very much.

I don't know about you, but things like that make me want to seek revenge. At times I even rehearse how I would do it and enjoy imagining how the person who hurt me would react. I have even entertained the idea of petitioning God for just five minutes to get even—just five measly minutes! But I know better. God has already told me what He thinks about that in His Word. The Bible plainly states in Romans 12:17-19,

"Do not repay anyone evil for evil. Be careful to do what is right in the eyes of everybody. If it is possible, as far as it depends on you, live at peace with everyone. Do not take revenge, my friends, but leave room for God's wrath, for it is written: 'It is mine to avenge. I will repay.'"

Do you ever wish there were some parts of the Bible you had never heard, so you wouldn't be accountable for them? This is one of mine. Paul went on to say that instead of retaliating we should give our enemy food and drink. He said by doing this we will "heap burning coals on his head" (Romans 12:20). Now I am all about dumping hot ashes on my enemy's head, but feeding her and giving her something to drink? I don't think so.

The words of 2 Corinthians 10:5b are very meaningful to me, "Take captive every thought to make it obedient to Christ." Most of the time we get it backwards. Instead of taking our thoughts captive we let our thoughts take us captive. Isn't it ironic that when we entertain the idea of revenge we are allowing ourselves to become hostages—prisoners of our own thoughts? You see, dwelling on retaliation is never obedient to Christ. It is the complete opposite.

Instead of seeking revenge, we are commanded—yes *commanded*—to forgive our enemies. Jesus said, "Love your enemies, do good to those who hate you, bless those who curse you, pray for those who mistreat you" (Luke 6:27-28). The disciple Peter had some specific questions about forgiveness for Jesus. He asked, "How many times shall I forgive my brother when he sins against me? Up to seven times?" Jesus told Peter that seventy times seven was how many times he had to forgive (Matthew 18:21-22). That was not what Peter wanted to hear! No doubt he thought he was being very generous by offering seven times.

Sometimes we say, "I just don't feel like forgiving," and that's the truth. Rarely when we've been hurt do we feel like forgiving. But in reality, feelings have nothing to do with forgiveness. Waiting to *feel like* forgiving means it will never happen. Forgiving has to be an act of the will first.

That means we *choose* to forgive because we know it is the right thing to do. It's a daily decision to give up bitterness and resentment.

To help Peter understand forgiveness, Jesus gave him a parable (Matthew 18:23-35). It was about a servant who had been forgiven an exorbitant debt but wouldn't in turn forgive someone who owed him a very small amount. The point was this: God has forgiven us an exorbitant amount, and when we refuse to forgive one another, we become the unforgiving servant. Failure to forgive others shows a gross lack of appreciation for the price Jesus paid to forgive our sins.

In addition, Jesus said that there is a very practical reason to forgive. Do you know what it is? He said we must forgive so He can forgive us. Our forgiving others goes hand-in-hand with His forgiving us. "For if you forgive men when they sin against you, your heavenly Father will also forgive you. But if you do not forgive men their sins, your Father will not forgive your sins" (Matthew 6:14-15).

Do you really believe that in order to be forgiven, you have to forgive? I mean, really? Then why do you sulk when someone hurts you or someone you love? Behaving like a wounded animal is not going to help. Get up! Get over it! Choose to forgive. Escape the prison of unforgiveness and revenge! "Forgive as the Lord forgave you" (Colossians 3:13b).

Dear God,
This is such a challenging lesson. It's so hard to forgive people when they intentionally hurt us or someone we love. Sometimes the desire to get even almost consumes us. Our world even tells us that it is the right thing to do. Help us to keep in our minds the greatness of our own sins and the incredible price You paid to forgive us. Soften our hearts. Help us extend to others the grace You have so lovingly given to us.

In Jesus' Name,
Amen

Chapter 32

Snake in the Bush

"The one who is in you is greater than the one who is in the world."
—1 John 4:4b

Scripture Reading
Genesis 3

"Strange, very strange," we thought as we watched the birds while eating lunch one Sunday after church. Normally, the little swallows followed a very predictable routine as they munched on seeds from the bird feeder just outside our breakfast room window. First, they fly to a large oak tree and check for any sign of danger. From there they fly to a nearby bush at the corner of the house. If the coast is clear there, they make a beeline for the feeder.

On this particular Sunday, their behavior was much different. For some unknown reason their regular flight pattern from the oak tree to the bush was repeatedly diverted. Normally, it was a quick, uneventful flight. However, we observed that just as they approached the bush they would freeze for a second in midair, flutter their wings, and frantically fly away.

Finally Waylon said, "Look at those silly birds."

"Something is wrong," I said, getting up from the table. When I opened the door and looked outside, I saw that something was wrong all right. A four-foot black snake was coiled up in the bush. "No wonder you poor little birds are frightened," I sympathized. "I would be frightened too." Actually, I *was* frightened.

Prior to that day the bush had always provided a refuge for the birds—a place to hide from a predator such as this. When they saw the snake lurking in the bush, their God-given instinct prompted them to flee, and fast. Nothing in the bird feeder was worth risking an encounter with the predator in the bush. How clever—actually, how cruel—that the snake would pick the very place where the birds normally felt safe to set up an ambush.

Doesn't this story remind you of Satan? Right off the bat in Genesis 3, another snake, the serpent in the Garden of Eden, is described as "crafty." Don't think for a minute that he didn't know exactly where Eve felt safe and secure. He knew every move of her daily routine. He was stealthily positioning himself where he could have the greatest opportunity to catch Eve off-guard. Unfortunately, Eve did not perceive him as a "snake in the bush" or respond the way our feathered friends did. Instead, she engaged in what seemed to be a harmless, friendly conversation, not realizing her danger.

The snake's conversation was carefully orchestrated with a hidden agenda designed to cast doubt about God—who He is, what He had said, and what His motives were. Very subtly, the snake set Eve up to make the worst mistake of her life. He undermined everything that God had said—everything that would ensure happiness and security for Eve and her husband in the Garden of Eden.

How frightening it is to think that Satan is so smooth, so calculating, and so callous—that he takes pride in tempting us to make destructive choices that not only affect us but all those around us. How sad that Eve was clueless about the impact of what she had done until it was too late. It was not until she began to experience the devastating consequences of shame and guilt that she understood the serpent's cruel intent. Eve was deceived about the big price tag sin carries—one that not only she would pay but her family and others as well.

It is imperative for us to keep our heads up and our eyes open. We don't know what kind of trap Satan is setting for us nor what kind of disguise he will be wearing. He may appear as a snake in a bush, but more than likely he will be much more subtle, possibly masquerading as a wholesome, godly individual—"an angel of light" (2 Corinthians 11:14) as Paul described him.

Know for a fact that Satan chooses his prey carefully. That's why Peter reminded us that we must "be self-controlled and alert. Your enemy the devil prowls around like a roaring lion looking for someone to devour" (1 Peter 5:8).

Satan is real, and he is vicious. He is out to get you and will stop at nothing. But don't make the mistake of ascribing to him more power than he possesses. He is not omnipotent. God is. Remember, "The one who is in you is greater than the one who is in the world" (1 John 4:4b). No matter what disguises or tactics Satan chooses to use against you today, make sure that you claim the promise that God will always be with you and will never abandon you (Joshua 1:5).

Take comfort that God knows when and where you are vulnerable. As surely as He tenderly cares for the tiny swallows in my backyard, He will take care of you also. God gave swallows instincts for their protection, and He has empowered you with His Spirit to stand firmly against the enemy. "Be strong in the Lord and in his mighty power. Put on the full armor of God so that you can take your stand against the devil's schemes" (Ephesians 6:10-11).

Dear Father,
I realize that I am vulnerable, but I know that You are able and willing to help me stand firm against the temptations and attacks of Satan. Let me be aware of Satan's reality today, but help me claim the victory that is mine because of Your reality.

In the Powerful Name of Jesus,
Amen

Chapter 33

Proud Mama

"Her children arise and call her blessed."
—Proverbs 31:28a

Scripture Reading
Deuteronomy 6:4-25

"O say, can you see, by the dawn's early light, what so proudly we hail'd at the twilight's last gleaming" and on she sang until she belted out, "O'er the land of the free and the home of the brave."

Talk about proud—I was a proud mama. I wanted to stand up and say, "Hey, y'all, that's my baby girl, my Emily, standing at center court singing the national anthem. And do you realize it's being televised on ESPN?" But I didn't say a word. Instead I just beamed.

I was so focused on and enamored with Emily that I lost touch with my surroundings. About halfway through "The Star-Spangled Banner" I noticed that everyone was turned around backwards—everyone except me. I thought, "What is wrong with these people? Why would they turn their back on someone singing the national anthem? How unpatriotic can you get?" But not wanting to miss a note of the song or even blink lest I miss something—I was savoring every moment—I thought perhaps I could figure it out later.

When Emily finished singing everyone immediately turned back around to face the court. It was then I realized that sometimes a proud mama can overdo it. Glancing over my shoulder I discovered that the American flag was waving right behind me. Normally, that would have embarrassed me to death, but not that night. The only reason I had driven to the Pete Maravich Assembly Center at Louisiana State University was to see and hear Emily sing. There was no way I could've turned my back on that precious child—not even for Old Glory.

We always knew that Em would be some type of performer. From the time she was able to walk, talk and dress herself, she loved to be in costume—either her big sister's clothes or just a piece of fabric draped around her body. She spent countless hours standing on the hearth entertaining pretend audiences until her debut at age eight. Dressed as a firefly she sang "This Little Light of Mine" at the top of her lungs. She was so cute! Little did we know then that God would give her the opportunity to stand before live audiences singing in musicals and basketball arenas.

Children. The Bible says they are a blessing from the Lord (Psalm 127:3). And that they are. However, sometimes it just doesn't seem like it. Frequently we have to search for the blessing part. Often, being a mother is a much bigger job than we signed up for. The job description changes and expands almost daily.

Early on, I had my doubts whether I was cut out to be a mother. To be honest, after a three-month bout with postpartum depression, I didn't know whether I had what it took to do the job. However, when my colicky baby turned into a cooing, smiling, and sleeping baby, things looked much different.

Putting My Dress-Up Clothes Away

Twelve consecutive years of Sesame Street and Mr. Rogers were tough. There were days when I thought that perhaps working would be much more rewarding. I used to jokingly say to Waylon, "I want a job where I can wear high-heeled shoes and carry a briefcase." So one year for Christmas Waylon gave me a briefcase. He said he knew I already had the high heels.

My heart's desire has always been to be a good mother. I heard John Maxwell say that our goal in life should be "for those who know us best to respect us the most." I never wanted the girls to see me as one person at church and quite a different one at home. I'm sure there were days when my walk didn't match my talk, but I pray those days were the exception rather than the rule. And on those days when my behavior was not consistent with what I taught the girls, I'm so thankful that they loved me in spite of myself. How comforting it is to know that "love covers over a multitude of sins" (1 Peter 4:8b).

Looking back on the years when the girls were growing up, I realize that I could have done many things differently and been a better mother. But you know what? I can't go back and do any of those things over. Whatever was done was done. Those pages have been written in indelible ink.

Many people believe that parenting, like golf, includes a "mulligan." In golf, a mulligan is a shot that is so bad you decide it doesn't count, and it's not added to the score. It's like the shot never happened. Unfortunately, in parenting there are no mulligans. Everything we do counts. Everything we do has an impact. While there are times when God gives us opportunities to redo some things and get them right the second time, the first time was not a mulligan. There are still consequences that go with it. Besides, there's not always a chance for a do-over. That's why the best thing we can do as parents is to listen to what Paul said in Colossians 3:17 when he advised, "And whatever you do, whether in word or deed, do it all in the name of the Lord Jesus." All our parenting, whether we have young children, teenagers, or adult children, should be done prayerfully, seeking

God's will in all our relationships.

The Bible places the responsibility of teaching our children about God squarely on the shoulders of parents. In Deuteronomy 6:7-9, the writer instructs parents to tell their children about God all through the day from the time they get up until they go to sleep at night. Talking about God and spiritual matters ought to be as natural as talking about what's for dinner. Proverbs 22:6 tells parents to "Train a child in the way he should go, and when he is old he will not turn from it." The writer emphasized how important those formative years are in the life of a child. In Ephesians 6:4, Paul told parents, actually fathers, "Do not exasperate your children; instead, bring them up in the training and instruction of the Lord." I don't know how many fathers are reading this book, but if you are a father, I want to beg you to take your God-given role seriously. I grew up without a father in the home, and in some ways I feel cheated. I wish I knew the feeling of having a daddy hold me in his arms and tell me about God. And don't forget the first part where Paul reminded you dads not to be harsh or unreasonable with your children (good advice for moms too). Be tender with your children. Listen to them. They want you to hear what they say as much as you want them to hear what you say.

Parenting truly is an awesome responsibility—a relentless 24/7 job with no time off. We must not take it lightly, because there's a little boy or a little girl depending on us to do it right. As we raise them we are either setting them up to succeed or to fail. While they will be held accountable for their choices when they grow up, we will be held accountable for how well we equipped them to make those choices.

In describing the godly woman, Proverbs 31:28a says, "Her children arise and call her blessed." Let me ask you a very sobering question—how would your children describe you? When they become adults and can look back on their childhood, what will they say about you? Will they rise up and call you blessed?

Dear Lord,

What an awesome blessing it is to be a mother. It is a privilege for You to entrust one of Your precious little ones into my hands. Because there are no mulligans in parenting, please guide me so I can be a good steward of the lives You have placed under my influence and authority.

In Jesus' Name,
Amen

Chapter 34

The Ugliest Dress I've Ever Seen

"I also want women to dress modestly, with decency and propriety, not with braided hair or gold or pearls or expensive clothes, but with good deeds, appropriate for women who profess to worship God."
—1 Timothy 2:9-10

Scripture Reading
1 Peter 3:1-6

There she stood, my dream-child girl in my dream-child dress—a navy blue sailor dress with a white collar, red tie, black patent-leather shoes, and red tights—posing for her first real portrait. Anna was absolutely adorable. I knew choosing a pose for the portrait was going to be difficult. But after days of "Should we pick this one?" or "Should we pick that one?" we finally made our selection.

When Anna outgrew the sailor dress, I carefully wrapped it in tissue paper and tucked it away in hopes that there might be another little girl to wear it. Sure enough, five and a half years later another baby girl

Putting My Dress-Up Clothes Away

named Emily was born into our family. I could hardly wait for her to turn four so we could have her portrait taken in the same dream-child dress.

Having seen her sister's portrait hanging in the family room for four years, Emily couldn't wait to have her own. Finally the day arrived, and I reached into the closet to get the dress for the portrait. I unwrapped it carefully as Emily asked, "What's that?"

"Why, it's the dress you're going to have your portrait made in so we can have a picture just like Anna's," I answered with excitement in my voice. Realizing by the look on her face that Emily was not nearly as excited, I asked, "What do you think?"

Without batting an eye she said, "I think that is the ugliest dress I have ever seen!"

"Oh no," I argued, "It's beautiful, and you are going to look just like sister."

"But I don't like that dress," she protested.

"Well, just wear it today for your picture. Then we'll take it off." Seeing that I wasn't going to give in, she reluctantly put the dress on, obviously not a happy camper.

Although Emily tried to comply with the photographer's requests, she could not conceal her disappointment over having to wear the sailor dress. Finally after about a dozen or so shots I thanked the photographer, knowing that we would be lucky to have one decent pose. Surprisingly there were several but none of them the real Emily—neither her expressions nor her smile.

Realizing that I had made a big mistake as a parent, I said, "Emily, Mama shouldn't have forced you to wear Anna's dress for your portrait. I'm sorry. We are going to do it over, and this time you can pick out the dress."

"Really?" she asked with a big grin on her face.

"Really," I replied, "This time you can choose any Sunday dress that you want." So off she flew in a flash to her room.

In a few minutes she happily returned with the dress she wanted to wear. It was an Emily dress if there ever was one—a fussy, frilly pastel aqua blue dress with no telling how many yards of lace on it. We quickly put the dress on and went to the studio.

As I watched her pose I knew the outcome was going to be quite different this time. It was obvious that she felt good about herself. She was beautiful with her long flowing blond curls and frilly aqua dress on, smiling from ear to ear and cocking her head at just the right angles—enough to steal anyone's heart.

As I look at those portraits, my treasures hanging in the family room, I am so thankful that I don't have two little girls in sailor dresses. Instead I have two little girls in dresses that reflect not only their beauty but their personality and taste as well—just the way God made them. Anna to this day prefers tailored clothing while Emily prefers more frilly attire.

While there are many applications for this story, I want to use it to talk about how we dress. Does it matter to God whether we wear a tailored navy sailor dress or a frilly aqua blue one with yards and yards of lace? I don't think so. But don't think for a minute that it doesn't matter to God how we dress. It does. Is there a certain way a godly woman should or should not dress? I think there is. Paul told Timothy, a young minister, to encourage the women in his congregation at Ephesus to "dress modestly, with decency and propriety" (1 Timothy 2:9). What does "modestly with decency and propriety" mean? In Paul's day it meant for a woman neither to become obsessed with how she looked—her wardrobe and accessories—nor to use her freedom in Christ to dress inappropriately. Paul wrote, "I also want women to dress modestly, with decency and propriety, not with braided hair or gold or pearls or expensive clothes, but with good deeds, appropriate for women who profess to worship God" (1 Timothy 2:9-10).

In Corinth, Paul told the men to cut their hair and the women not to

(1 Corinthians 11:5-7). Doesn't that sound strange? Why in the world would Paul issue such a mandate? The answer has to do with culture. In that day long hair on men and short hair on women was considered a sign of prostitution. The last thing a Christian needed to do in Corinth was to appear as a prostitute. It would have sent the wrong message (Life Application Bible, p. 2016).

Paul's admonition to "dress modestly, with decency and propriety" is especially pertinent in our sexually-charged, out-of-control culture where people's bodies are referred to as "eye candy," where lust, sexual immorality, and sexual crimes are epidemic. That's why I believe that as women we need to ask ourselves some serious questions about what we wear. For example, would this outfit please God? Would it send the wrong message in our culture? Does this outfit in any way make my intentions look questionable? Would another woman feel uncomfortable about the way I'm dressed in her husband's presence? Would this dress, top, pants, or whatever, tempt a man to lust?

I'm wondering if the word "underwear" will have to be deleted from the dictionary because what used to be worn under is now worn for outer garments. Women now wear in public what they used to wear in private. If you think I'm crazy, just look around and see how many women are at the mall, movies, or anywhere else wearing apparel that looks like pajamas. What are women thinking?

In the name of trying to look beautiful, many women have compromised being a lady by the clothing they either want to wear or feel pressured to wear. Women are being squeezed into the mold of this world through movies, television, and the fashion industry. I feel it just as much as you do. I struggle just like you trying to find something stylish, tasteful, and modest. It's just plain hard to shop these days. It's not nearly as much fun as it used to be. Although there aren't a lot of options for clothing, we must not let that be an excuse to dress in an ungodly manner.

Do you get the point? I fear that we are about to reach the point of no return when it comes to women's clothing. Let me close by asking you two simple questions: (1) What do you have in your closet that you wouldn't have worn five to ten years ago—that you would have considered inappropriate? (2) What younger woman is looking at you to see how a godly woman is supposed to be dressed?

Dear God,
Our society is so mixed up when it comes to priorities and values. Help us know how to dress in a way that we feel good about ourselves, but more importantly in a way that would honor You. Help us not to compromise by conforming to our world, but help us to maintain the standard You have set for us.

In Jesus' Name,
Amen

Chapter 35

Foolish Pride

"God opposes the proud but gives grace to the humble."
—1 Peter 5:5

Scripture Reading
2 Kings 5:1-14

What is it about human nature that makes us resist the simple? Why do we think that solutions to problems have to be expensive, time-consuming, and/or painful? Unfortunately, that mindset has been around a long time.

Let's consider a military man in the Old Testament by the name of Naaman, a highly regarded, valiant commander of the Syrian army. His story is found in 2 Kings 5:1-14. In spite of his virtues, Naaman had a serious problem—he had leprosy, a dreaded, incurable disease of his day. Though his leprosy must not have been debilitating at that point, since he still held his position, the long-term prognosis was fatal. Naaman could see the handwriting on the wall, and it was frightening (Life Application Bible, p. 623).

His greatest desire, no doubt, was to find a cure—somewhere, somehow. God had a cure waiting for him, but it wouldn't come in the way Naaman expected. Could he have imagined that two seemingly insignificant servants would be his ticket to life and health, and that the proposed treatment for his condition would be given to him in a foreign country by a local prophet?

Naaman had an Israelite servant girl. She told Naaman's wife about a prophet named Elisha who could heal Naaman of his leprosy. Naaman's wife quickly passed the word along to him. With the king's blessing, Naaman left Syria and headed to Samaria in pursuit of a possible cure for his incurable disease. Thinking that such treatment would surely be expensive, he loaded his horses and chariots with 750 pounds of silver, 150 pounds of gold, and 10 new outfits.

Being the distinguished commander that he was, he expected a certain protocol upon arriving in Samaria. Boy, was he shocked and insulted when the prophet, Elisha, didn't even come out to meet him! Instead, Elisha sent a messenger who told Naaman to go and immerse himself seven times in the Jordan River.

I can just imagine what Naaman must have thought. "He said for me to do *what*? What kind of quack is this? Do you mean to tell me that I have come all the way from Syria for someone to tell me that this dreaded disease can be cured by the murky water of the Jordan River? I'm not doing that! What kind of fool does he think I am? I'm looking for a real cure, not some kind of fool-hearted superstition! Seven times in the Jordan River—you've got to be kidding!" Off he went in a huff—just as he came—leprous and proud.

Leprous and proud. Leprous and proud. Leprous and proud. Do you see it? Naaman had two fatal diseases rather than one. He knew that his leprosy was terminal, but what he failed to acknowledge was the fact that his pride could be the cause of his death.

Pride is a deadly sin. God hates it (Proverbs 8:13b). We are repeatedly warned about its destructive power in Scripture: "Pride goes before destruction, a haughty spirit before a fall" (Proverbs 16:18). Wise is the person who watches for any sign of it in his life and allows the Holy Spirit to convict him of it—nipping it in the bud every time.

Let's look at the way God convicted Naaman of his pride. Who was instrumental in getting Naaman's attention? A lowly servant, again. It was a servant who began this process, and later it was a servant who attacked Naaman's real disease—pride. The servant said, in effect, "Look, man, if Elisha told you to do something difficult or expensive you would have done that with no questions asked. Why won't you do this simple thing he told you to do? What do you have to lose?" The Bible says, "So he [Naaman] went down and dipped himself in the Jordan seven times, as the man of God had told him, and his flesh was restored and became clean like that of a young boy" (2 Kings 5:14).

Let's take this story seriously. Could it be that we experience poor health and physical problems (and other problems for that matter) because we are too stubborn to do the simple things that we know to do or are prescribed to do? Let me give you a personal illustration.

A few years ago, I began to experience some pain down my right arm. I could hardly turn my head in any direction—up, down, or to either side. Thinking that I had a pulled muscle, I immediately went to the doctor. He thought it was a pulled muscle too, but when the pain grew more intense over time, I knew something else was wrong.

I decided to see a specialist, and he immediately ordered an MRI. The results were not good—two bulging discs and a bone spur. He recommended that I consider one of three options, not giving me much hope that the first two would work. He said I could try physical therapy, steroid injections, or surgery. Well, that was a no-brainer, at least for me. He said he would give me only six weeks in therapy before I would have to try more aggressive treatment.

I immediately went to a physical therapist, one in whom I have great confidence. I knew she would put me through the wringer, but I also knew she would do everything in her power to keep me from the other two options.

Sure enough, after reviewing the referral from the specialist, my therapist felt confident that I could deal with the problem without medication or surgery if I would do what she said—a daily regimen of exercise. That sounded great to me.

When I left her office the first day, I had some of the simplest exercises you have ever seen. In fact, her instructions were, "Don't overdo it!" I could have left that day saying, "What good is barely lifting my head ten times, five times a day going to do?" But I knew my therapist, and I trusted her. Besides, I was in bad shape. Anything was worth a try.

How easy it would have been to let my pride get in the way and to question my therapist's wisdom because what she prescribed was so simple! If I had, I would have been robbed of the three wonderful years I have just enjoyed.

While in this example I didn't let my pride win, I must confess to you that most of the time I do. In fact, it is a daily struggle to accept God's simple plan for abundant living. How easy it is to overlook the obvious in search of something more complicated and difficult!

The Bible says that our bodies are the temple of the Holy Spirit (1 Corinthians 6:19). The implication is that we are stewards of our bodies and that God expects us to take good care of them. Perhaps the story of Naaman is a wake-up call for you today. God has given us His Word to direct us through life. Why then do we let our pride keep us from His blessings? Remember, many problems in life have very simple solutions. Don't let your pride keep you from hearing what God is saying to you. "God opposes the proud but gives grace to the humble. Humble yourselves, therefore, under God's mighty hand, that he may lift you up in due time" (1 Peter 5:5-6). Listen to those precious servants He puts in your path today to help you.

Dear Heavenly Father,
Although I don't like to admit it, I often let my pride get in the way of doing what You want me to do. Sometimes I refuse to listen to people You place in my path to give me godly counsel. Forgive me, Lord. Help me to surrender my foolish pride to You and follow You in obedience.

In Jesus' Name,
Amen

Chapter 36

The White Out

"God is our refuge and strength, an ever-present help in trouble."
—Psalm 46:1

Scripture Reading
Psalm 139:1-12

A light snow had begun to fall just as we left Breckenridge, Colorado. After skiing with our family for several days Waylon and I were on our way to Beaver Creek to ski with some friends. As we made our way to Interstate 70, the snow was coming down hard. Being from South Louisiana where it snows every ten years if we're lucky, we proceeded cautiously toward our destination.

The farther west we drove, the harder it began to snow, and the more tense I became. But because I had my heart set on seeing our friends, I didn't say anything at first. Besides, I could tell this situation qualified as an adventure for Waylon. The thought of turning around never occurred to him. However, as the visibility decreased, the knot in my stomach increased. Finally when I could stand it no longer, I expressed my anxiety even though I knew Waylon was going to think I was a sissy. Obviously a bit perturbed, he asked if I wanted to turn around. Without blinking an eye, too frightened for words, I nodded my head. Waylon pulled off at the next exit.

We tried to reach our friends by cell phone but were unable to get through. With the conditions worsening by the second, we got back on the interstate and headed toward Breckenridge. By that time not only was it snowing quarter-sized flakes, but also the wind was blowing fiercely. Within minutes the roadway was completely blanketed with new-fallen snow concealing all the striping. And when I say all, I mean ALL. To make matters worse, heightening our anxiety, the windshield wipers froze and became inoperable. Talk about terrifying, it was terrifying! To top it all off, cars were zooming past us like the sun was shining in the middle of July.

By this time Waylon had joined his neurotic wife emotionally. He was scared too. Normally, he acts like Mr. Cool and assures me that everything is going to be fine, but on that stormy afternoon there were no reassuring words—only panic-stricken ones.

With the frozen wipers it soon became apparent to both of us that the only way we were going to be able to keep the car on the road was for me to stick my head out the window and verbally direct Waylon. Much to our surprise and relief we discovered that the shoulder of the road was marked with four-foot stakes about every fifty feet. Later we learned that the stakes were there for situations just like we found ourselves in. They were the only thing that enabled us to safely stay on the mountainous road.

By this time we had slowed to a snail's pace, but we knew that to stop completely would be the worst thing we could do. Our greatest fear was that we would rear-end someone who had done that very thing or be rear-ended ourselves. As we inched our way ever so slowly along I-70, I remember thinking, "Did Breckenridge change its geographical location while we were gone?" It seemed like an eternity since we had turned around. Then all of a sudden I looked up, and in a split second I realized that we had missed our exit—the huge green sign to Breckenridge. "Oh no!" I thought. "What do we do now?" I don't know whose crazy idea it was, but we decided to back up on the interstate. Was that dumb or what? We didn't care. We were desperate!

Although Waylon's vision couldn't have been any more impaired if he had been blindfolded, he safely maneuvered us off the interstate with my verbal assistance. (If you want to test the trust level in your marriage, put a blindfold on your husband and get out on the interstate. Then try directing him for the next thirty miles. If you live to tell about it and your marriage survives, you'll probably celebrate your fiftieth anniversary.)

We pulled into a nearby Kentucky Fried Chicken. It didn't matter what kind of joint it was; I just wanted to get off the road and out of the car before I hyperventilated or froze to death.

Getting out of the car, Waylon, visibly shaken but relieved, looked at me and said, "Martha, you amaze me. I can't believe how cool you were under such intense pressure." I don't have a clue what he expected me to say or do. Prepared or not for my reaction, I looked at him and started bawling like a baby. I must have cried for half an hour after we got inside the KFC. Everyone stared at us as if we were crazy. I didn't care. I was happy to be alive. I didn't care if I lived at the KFC for the rest of my life.

What we didn't know then, but later learned, was that this phenomenon is called a white out. Shortly after we headed toward Beaver Creek, the state police had closed the interstate. We were in a much more precarious situation than we even feared. If something had happened, no one would have known where we were—not to mention that we didn't have adequate food, water, or clothing to protect us from hypothermia.

But there was One who knew exactly where we were—the One who is so keenly aware of us that He "knows when I sit and when I rise" (Psalm 139:2). The One who sees my "going out and my lying down" (Psalm 139:3). The One who never lets me out of His sight. The One who "hems me in—behind and before" (Psalm 139:5). The One who takes His responsibility to care for me very seriously. And on that stormy day in the mountains of Colorado, He proved it.

Take heart today in knowing that God is always looking out for His children. There is no place you can go that will be out of His jurisdiction. "God is our refuge and strength, an ever-present help in trouble" (Psalm 46:1).

Lord,
Thank You so much that You don't need a GPS to know where I am and what's going on in my life. I am so thankful that there is nowhere I can go that You will not be with me. Thank You that You are my "refuge and strength, an ever-present help in trouble."

In Jesus' Name,
Amen

Chapter 37

Pooh Friends

"A friend loves at all times."
—Proverbs 17:17

Scripture Reading
Ecclesiastes 4:9-12

I am a Winnie the Pooh girl. The last year I taught fourth grade I decorated my room in a Pooh theme. When one of my colleagues asked if I didn't think Pooh was a little juvenile for fourth graders, I replied, "No, I don't. If you're too old for Winnie the Pooh, you are too old!"

Before Jake, our first grandson, was born, a friend said to me, "Martha, you need to have that baby call you Honey since you love Pooh so much." I took her up on it, and when Jake or Chase says, "Honey," it's like music to my ears. And my response usually is, "Whatever you want, baby!"

I could go on and on talking about Jake and Baby Chase, the two very special little boys in my life. However, what I really want to talk about is women and our need for girlfriends—Pooh Friends I call them. Let's face it—we need each other. Unfortunately our microwave society has robbed us of something that most of us so desperately need and crave.

Putting My Dress-Up Clothes Away

I love my husband dearly. But there are times when I talk to him about things that either bother or excite me, and I can tell he just doesn't get it. It's not that he doesn't want to or try to—it's just that he is a man and sees things through a totally different paradigm. That's why we need a girlfriend who will cry with us (on cue), laugh with us, miserabilize with us (I know that's not a word, but you get what I mean), fight for us, defend us, not to mention shop with us, and a thousand other things. So if girlfriends are that important, let's talk about some characteristics of a Pooh Friend.

A Pooh Friend will comfort you on a blustery day. We all have those days and sometimes they seem to come one after the other. A PF (short for Pooh Friend) will listen to you and encourage you on the days when you feel like Eeyore's twin or when you've eaten too much and can't get into your jeans. She knows just when to drop by with homemade cookies (Yes, slice and bake or break-apart ones do qualify), send a card, fax or email a Scripture, deliver a bouquet of flowers, or encourage you to eat something chocolate.

I remember a time when I was having a very blustery day and a PF called. She innocently asked how I was doing, and it was like Niagara Falls broke loose. I took several minutes to regain my composure. But because she is a Pooh Friend she listened to me and loved me over the phone. Later I told her it was just "one of those days" and a call from a telemarketer may have evoked the same response.

Let me just say one thing before I go any further (Shh! Don't tell)—husbands are sometimes not good PFs because they like to fix everything. And as you girls well know, sometimes fixing the situation is *not* what we want. We just want to talk about it, and about it, and about it. Right? I knew you would agree.

A PF will also let you be yourself—bouncy or unbouncy. She will let you run around like a chicken with your head chopped off like Rabbit, let you be clingy like Piglet, let you be down in the dumps like Eeyore, or let you bounce off the walls like Tigger. What's neat about her is she knows you are special—just the way God made you to be. Like Tigger, she knows the most wonderful thing about you is that you're the only one.

The thing that is so comforting about a PF is she doesn't expect you to be perfect. She sees you mess up big time and loves you anyway. No matter whether you're wallowing in the mud, lost in the misty forest, or running from a swarm of bees, it doesn't faze her. She's in the relationship for the long haul—there's nothing "fair weather" about her.

However, a genuine PF will also tell you when you are out of control. If you have a meltdown and try to rationalize it, a Pooh Friend won't hesitate to reprimand you. She can get on your case, but you listen to her knowing she always looks out for your best interest.

You know you can trust a PF because she has integrity which is characterized by honesty and sincerity, not to be confused with brutality. Some women say they are being honest when they are just being mean.

A Pooh Friend is loyal. With her your back is as safe as your front. Because she values your relationship she will protect and defend you when necessary. Betrayal couldn't be farther from her mind.

You can trust a Pooh Friend. She is the "real deal"—not a knock-off who can and will hurt you in a heartbeat. A PF understands confidentiality and treasures the fact that you would bare your soul to her.

A Pooh Friend doesn't play games in her relationships. You always know where you stand with her. (Don't you just hate it when you have to play "Guess What's Wrong with Suzie?") There's nothing more painful and aggravating than a relationship in which everyone feels like they are walking on eggshells.

A Pooh Friend will forgive you. She won't hold a grudge—at least not for long. She won't give you a cold shoulder and pout for weeks. If she does, she'll ask you to forgive her because real friends can't have a wedge

Putting My Dress-Up Clothes Away

in their relationship without feeling miserable about it.

A Pooh Friend has a positive outlook on life. She might be Eeyore from time to time but not as a general rule. She knows Eeyores get heavy and tend to hinder rather than nurture a friendship.

When you are feeling "a little eleven o'clockish," a PF is fun to go to lunch with or have a turkey sandwich with while sitting at the kitchen counter. Conversation comes quite naturally because you just pick up where you left off the last time the two of you were together. And when it's time to leave you won't be finished either, but that's okay. You just quote Tigger and say "TTFN—ta-ta for now."

Pooh Friends have lots of room in their hearts for other friends. They aren't possessive. They don't hold you so close that they suffocate you nor do they get mad when they don't have all of your attention. I once received a card from a sweet friend. It had a picture of Piglet and Pooh on the front. Piglet was asking, "You have lots of friends, don't you, Pooh?" And on the inside Pooh lovingly answered, "Yes, I do, but only one Piglet." Pooh Friends have lots of friends in their "Hundred Acre Wood."

Perhaps one of the most important characteristics of a PF, though, is that she is one who will nail your tail back on when you lose it. I love the story about Eeyore losing his tail and all his friends helping him search for it. I once had a set of note cards with a picture of Christopher Robin surrounded by all the friends nailing Eeyore's tail back on, and the caption read, "Friendship is such a comforting sort of thing." And it is. Quite often I need someone to nail my tail back on. In fact, I have lost it so many times that my friends now have to attach it with a molly bolt! But they don't mind. They never let me down. Instead they just say, "Silly old Martha," knowing that sooner or later they will have to do it again. And it's such a comforting sort of thing.

The Bible tells us how valuable friendships are, especially when the friends know the Lord. "Two are better than one.... If one falls down, his friend can help him up. But pity the man who falls and has no one to help him up! ... A cord of three strands is not quickly broken" (Ecclesiastes 4:9-10, 12b).

I probably could go on for days talking about Pooh Friends. I am blessed because I have many. There are ladies I can call anytime day or night with the deepest needs or joys of my heart. They are always there for me—just as the Bible promises: "A friend loves at all times" (Proverbs 17:17). Thank you, my precious Pooh Friends. I love you so much.

Just one more thing if you don't mind my asking—do you have a Pooh Friend?—I mean just one person you can really count on? I hope you do. But remember, a friendship is a reciprocal relationship. In order to *have* a Pooh Friend you have to *be* a Pooh Friend. Why not pause right now and either thank God for your Pooh Friend or ask Him to give you one?

Dear God,
I can't thank You enough for my precious friends. Only You know how they have stood by my side through the good times and the bad. They have held my hands up when I was too weak to do it myself. My friends have been just as quick to stand by my side and rejoice with my family during the happy times. Often I've looked at them during the memorable occasions, and it seemed that they couldn't have been any happier if my celebration had been theirs. What a blessing! Because I'm a minister's wife they know that being my friend is a little tricky, but they also know You have placed them in my life to support, love, and sustain me. Thank You, Lord Jesus. Help me to be their friend as well. Please help me to know when they need me and how I can be their friend that loves at all times.

In Jesus' Name,
Amen

Chapter 38

"Honey, You Must Need a New Battery"

> "Let us not become weary in doing good, for at the proper time we will reap a harvest if we do not give up."
> —Galatians 6:9

Scripture Reading
1 Corinthians 9:24-27

Jake, my three-year-old grandson, sat in the back seat making a guttural sound that he called "the pig noise." After a few minutes, he said, "Honey, *you* make the pig noise this time."

I relished the thought that my grandson assumed I could do anything. But knowing he would love me just as much when he realized I couldn't, I replied, "Jake, Honey can't make the pig noise."

Puzzled by my apparent inability to perform such a simple task, Jake sat silently in the back seat analyzing the problem. Then, with the genius of Albert Einstein (remember, he is my grandson), he exclaimed very confidently, "Honey, you must need a new battery!" It was a no-brainer to him.

"Yes, Jake, Honey does need a new battery!" I agreed whole-heartedly, chuckling to myself trying not to insult the conclusion he had drawn. Then I thought, "Child, if you only knew how badly Honey needs a new battery!"

What about you? Do you need a new battery? Do you ever feel like your energy is depleted or that you have lost your enthusiasm? Well, congratulations! Welcome to the real world. It's a feeling we all experience from time to time. That's why Paul told the Galatians, "Let us not become weary in doing good, for at the proper time we will reap a harvest if we do not give up" (Galatians 6:9). You see, he knew that running out of steam and giving up can be a difficulty for us all.

Paul understood that becoming a Christian is exciting, but he also knew how difficult it is to persevere through the daily grind. He wanted his readers to see the big picture and not lose sight of the ultimate goal—the harvest. Let's think about it this way. Would it make sense to do all the backbreaking work that is required to plant a garden, and then later say, "I'm tired. I don't feel like picking all that stuff"? No, we would push it into overdrive and make sure we got the reward for all our hard work.

In 1 Corinthians, Paul compared life to a race. He suggested that it is just as absurd for a Christian to quit serving God as it would be for a marathon runner to quit before he finished the race. It's not that many of us haven't worked hard in our walk with the Lord. It's just that we get tired at times, and the thought of quitting seems so appealing. But Paul would say, "No way! You got into this race and you must finish it—and finish it well." He would encourage us to run the race with perseverance and receive the prize waiting for us just over the finish line.

Shortly after our younger daughter, Emily, was born, I entered a 5K race at New Orleans Seminary where we were living at the time. It wasn't a big deal—just something to do on the Fourth of July. There weren't even many participants—just me and a few kids ten to fifteen years younger than I. Although my legs weren't old at that time, they were no competition for the younger ones. For them it was a "fun run" around our neighborhood. They jogged along, merrily carrying on a lively conversation, hardly breaking a sweat. Me? No conversation, lots of sweat, and heavily labored breathing—legs aching more with each step. It was no "fun run" to say the least.

As we were coming down the home stretch, which went right by my house, I distinctly remember thinking, "I'll just jog through my front door and grab a Twinkie on the way to the couch." But then my thoughts turned to what people might say. Certain that my friends would never let me live it down, I continued the race—and finished—LAST! Oh well, at least I had the consolation of knowing that I did the best I could. And I had the satisfaction of knowing that I didn't quit. I finished the race.

Life is a race. It's a marathon—not a sprint. It requires energy and perseverance. The temptation to quit is ever-present. But Christians must not quit; we must "press on....forgetting what is behind and straining toward what is ahead...to win the prize for which God has called me [us] heavenward in Christ Jesus" (Philippians 3:12-14).

What a wonderful consolation it must have been for Paul when he reached the end of his life and could confidently say, "The time has come for my departure. I have fought the good fight, I have finished the race, I have kept the faith. Now there is in store for me a crown of righteousness, which the Lord, the righteous Judge, will award to me on that day—and not only to me, but also to all who have longed for his appearing" (2 Timothy 4:6b-8).

I recently attended the funeral of a friend's father. He was a godly man. He exemplified a life that was lived all the way to the finish line. A few days before he passed away, knowing that death can be a terrifying experience for many people, the hospice nurse called him by name and asked him, "Are you worried or anxious about anything?"

Though ravaged with cancer and almost too weak to speak, he shook his head and said, "No, I'm eager." What a wonderful testimony! What about you—when it comes your time to leave this world will you be able to say, "I'm eager?"

Don't become weary in doing good. Don't throw in the towel. Hang in there because there's a great reward waiting for you at the finish line. "Therefore, since we are surrounded by such a great cloud of witnesses, let us throw off everything that hinders and the sin that so easily entangles, and let us run with perseverance the race marked out for us. Let us fix our eyes on Jesus, the author and perfecter of our faith, who for the joy set before him endured the cross, scorning its shame, and sat down at the right hand of the throne of God. Consider him who endured such opposition from sinful men, so that you will not grow weary and lose heart" (Hebrews 12:1-3).

Dear Father,
Sometimes we feel overwhelmed at how hard life is. Many days it's not a "fun run." Instead, it threatens to sap every ounce of strength we have. During those times, enable us to hear Your whispers of encouragement so that we can run the race with perseverance and receive the prize waiting for us just over the finish line.

In Jesus' Name,
Amen

Chapter 39

A Bouquet for Jesus

"Whatever you do, do it all for the glory of God."
—1 Corinthians 10:31

Scripture Reading
Ephesians 3:14-21

Well, here we are at our destination. For me it has been one of the most exciting yet taxing experiences I have ever had. While there are still so many experiences I would like to write about, this is where we must go our separate ways. I want to close by sharing a story that has profoundly touched my life.

The story is about an incredible Dutch woman who risked her life to hide Jews from the Nazis during World War II. For four years in a secret room in their home built by underground supporters, Corrie ten Boom and her family successfully housed and protected Jews from the German Gestapo.

But in February of 1944, Corrie, along with her father and three siblings, was arrested and taken to prison. Corrie spent four months in solitary confinement, surviving on meager rations and the comfort found in the four Gospels, which had been smuggled to her by a camp hospital nurse. Through reading of the sufferings of Jesus, Corrie was reminded and convinced that all the suffering she was enduring was not in vain—surely God had a purpose for it all. During this awful ordeal, Corrie was interrogated many times, allowing her to witness in a very innocent way while touching the lives of many who guarded her.

Four months after their first imprisonment, Corrie and her sister Betsie were moved by train to a labor camp in southern Holland. Three months later they were relocated to Ravensbruck, a German concentration camp. Life there was miserable for the 35,000 female prisoners. The accommodations were deplorable. Corrie and her sister were two of 1,400 inmates who were housed in a cold, damp, flea-infested barracks which was built to accommodate 400. Ironically the infestation proved to be a blessing in disguise. Not wanting to contend with the fleas, the guards left the inmates unsupervised at night. Consequently, it was possible for Corrie and Betsie to worship and pray with the other inmates using a Dutch Bible that had been smuggled to Corrie.

After three months of cruel treatment and inhumane living conditions, Betsie died. Corrie, however, was miraculously released, later discovering that her release had been a clerical mistake. Shortly afterwards all the women her age in the camp were murdered.

After the war, Corrie spent the next thirty years of her life fulfilling a vision that her sister Betsie had while in prison—a vision of operating a large house to rehabilitate those victimized by the Holocaust. One evening after the war, a man asked to shake Corrie's hand. She recognized him as one of the former SS guards at the camp. Although reluctant at first, Corrie knew that forgiveness would be her only path to restoration. "She later wrote about how important forgiveness was. In her rehabilitation work with victims of the Holocaust and other camp survivors, she found that only those who were able to forgive could make a good recovery and begin to live again." (Information for this story was drawn from *The Secret Room*, by David Wallington.)

News of Corrie's imprisonment and post-war rehabilitation efforts spread around the world, affording her many opportunities to share the love and providence of God with millions of people. When asked one day how she remained humble with all the praise and recognition she had received, she replied, "I accept every compliment as a flower and say thank you, and each evening I put them in a bunch and lay them at Jesus' feet, where the praise belongs" (quote drawn from *15 Minutes of Peace with God*, by Emilie Barnes).

What a remarkable story! I think it is one of the most inspiring ones I've ever read. Using Corrie ten Boom as my role model, I want to say that each chapter in this book is a flower, and now that we have reached the end, I want to put them all in a bouquet and lay them at the feet of Jesus where they rightfully belong. Not one of the stories in this book is my own doing. They exist because God saw fit to let me experience them while showing me a spiritual application for each one. I praise Him for that and for allowing me to write a book that would give Him glory.

"Now to him who is able to do immeasurably more than all we ask or imagine, according to his power that is at work within us, to him be glory in the church and in Christ Jesus throughout all generations, for ever and ever! Amen."
—*Ephesians 3:20-21*